CUTTING YOURSELF ON THE INSIDE

TIPS TO IDENTIFY AND OVERCOME ANOREXIA NERVOSA FOR TEEN GIRLS

SHANNON MICHELLE

TABLE OF CONTENTS

Introduction vii

1. UNDERSTANDING ANOREXIA NERVOSA 1
   What Is Anorexia Nervosa? 2
   Sight vs Weight 11

2. FAMILY DYNAMICS 15
   Parents or Guardians 16
   Father Figures 19
   Extended Family 22
   Siblings 24

3. FRIENDSHIPS 28
   Born to Be Different? 28
   Distant Friends 31
   Social Media 33
   True Friends 38

4. SIGNIFICANT OTHERS 40
   Romantic Challenges 41
   Healing Through Love Languages 49

5. SCHOOL AND EXTRACURRICULAR ACTIVITIES 52
   Sports 53
   Cheerleading 57
   Creativity 59
   Academic Clubs or Courses 62
   Community Projects 63
   Government, Leadership, and Media 65
   Religious Groups 67
   Part-Time Jobs 68
   Spare Time 69

6. TREATMENT 71
   Asking For Help 71
   Professional Support 73

Self-Help	81
Recovery	83
7. BLANK SLATE	87
A Healthy Relationship With Food	89
Your Brilliant Body	91
Afterword	93
Bibliography	95

© **Copyright 2022 - All rights reserved.**

The content contained within this book may not be reproduced, duplicated or transmitted without direct written permission from the author or the publisher.

Under no circumstances will any blame or legal responsibility be held against the publisher, or author, for any damages, reparation, or monetary loss due to the information contained within this book, either directly or indirectly.

Legal Notice:

This book is copyright protected. It is only for personal use. You cannot amend, distribute, sell, use, quote or paraphrase any part, or the content within this book, without the consent of the author or publisher.

Disclaimer Notice:

Please note the information contained within this document is for educational and entertainment purposes only. All effort has been executed to present accurate, up to date, reliable, complete information. No warranties of any kind are declared or implied. Readers acknowledge that the author is not engaged in the rendering of legal, financial, medical or professional advice. The content within this book has been derived from various sources. Please consult a licensed professional before attempting any techniques outlined in this book.

By reading this document, the reader agrees that under no circumstances is the author responsible for any losses, direct or indirect, that are incurred as a result of the use of the information contained within this document, including, but not limited to, errors, omissions, or inaccuracies.

INTRODUCTION

Have you ever looked in the mirror and felt unhappy with what you see? Do you have a difficult relationship with food, seeing it as a tool to control your appearance and mood? If you do, then I want you to know that you are not alone. There are sadly millions of teen girls out there, just like you, who are also struggling with these thoughts and feelings, and it may mean that you have an eating disorder called anorexia nervosa.

Eating disorders affect approximately 30 million people living in the United States alone and they are the third most common chronic illness among adolescent females (Rehman, 2022), yet many of these conditions are misunderstood. Fortunately, I am here to support and encourage you to address and get through any self-esteem, motivational, or eating challenges that have led you to anorexia nervosa and come out the other side as a winner.

My name is Shannon, and I am an anorexia nervosa and bulimia survivor. At the age of 12, I moved to Gainesville, Florida with my family and did all the normal things a growing young woman would do, attending Santa Fe Community College and then graduating to the University of Florida. As I was growing up, I channeled all of my energy into my studies and excelled academically, made a lot of friends, and maintained a good relationship with my then boyfriend. I was a cheerleader, and my boyfriend was the captain of the football team, so some would say that I was "living the dream," but during this seemingly positive time, I was struggling internally. Despite being popular, successful, and having a great social life, I was often on autopilot and felt as though the people around me didn't necessarily know who I really was inside. I then realized that I was hiding a pretty huge secret that went on to change my life in ways I could never have imagined: I was battling two of the most difficult eating disorders and didn't even know it! At my worst, I plummeted to just 92 pounds while struggling with self-worth, had a poor relationship with food, and constantly worried about external perceptions, but it wasn't until I was in high school that I realized my mental challenges had a name.

In one of my psychology classes, we were given a textbook to study. It had a chapter about eating disorders in it and as I began to read through it, I noticed that so many of the symptoms described rang true for me and I could relate to a lot of the case studies too. The alarm bells in my head instantly became deafening and my stomach churned as I realized that I had finally found something I could relate to and explained how I was feeling, right there in black and white. I had always known that something wasn't right in my mind, but it wasn't until this moment that something clicked, and it was a real 'eureka' moment for me! "I am suffering from anorexia nervosa," I said, and from that moment, I went on a difficult yet rewarding journey of self-discovery and healing.

Since leaving high school with an official diagnosis, I have spoken to friends and family about how I was feeling and have managed to slowly but surely improve my habits, body, and mindset by enrolling in therapy. I personally waited many years to address my struggles with anorexia this way, but I encourage all sufferers to try therapy as soon as you notice any symptoms, as it will help you heal at a younger age and live the majority of your life in a healthier way.

Fast-forward to today and I now want to use what I've learnt through my own recovery to support you in your journey toward getting out of the grips of anorexia too. I want to steer you away from the damage it can cause to your physical, mental, and emotional health and help you to eventually join me in living a free, happy, and fulfilling life. Now, I am not a professional doctor or therapist, but I have firsthand experience and knowledge that I will use to guide you in a way that is honest and caring. Having gone through it myself, I also understand how your self-esteem, school, friends, family, and romantic relationships can all affect your experience of anorexia and I know that my input and tips will greatly benefit young teens, like yourself. Think of me as your big sister who has been there, done that, and got the T-shirt–a T-shirt that I hope other girls never need to wear again.

CUTTING YOURSELF ON THE INSIDE

During my therapy sessions, I described the way I was feeling and the damage I was causing to my body as "cutting myself on the inside." This was because I found anorexia so internally painful that it felt like a form of inner self-harm. When I felt low, I would lose my appetite and cause myself pain by not eating, but the hunger pains and growls in my stomach also gave me a temporary sense of calm–a typical manifestation of self-harm–and this cycle would continue to repeat itself. The physical pain, along with the mental trauma and reasons I had for putting my body through this, seemed invisible and unfathomable to others. It felt like I was cleverly concealing my illness. People didn't seem to notice, or if they did, they didn't say anything, so I just kept going.

This silence around anorexia and other eating disorders that make you lose weight is sadly quite common. They are rarely discussed openly because it is usually considered a taboo subject. This could be because of their links to mental health or because society generally values smaller bodies. For example, in the late 1990s, being very slim with minimal curves and youthful features was seen as an ideal female body shape, and now, even with the Kim Kardashians and Cardi Bs of the world, being curvy is fine, as long as you are still slim in all the 'right' places. Furthermore, having a slender body has been a goal for so many women for so long, that when those suffering from anorexia lose weight, very few bat an eyelid or it will be left unaddressed until it becomes very severe. If eating disorders are addressed however, they are often made light of, with people telling sufferers to "just eat something" or that they should "feel happy about being slim," but this can be so unhelpful and even detrimental to recovery. This is why it is so important to open up the conversation and speak frankly about why these dangerous disorders can't be cured by simply eating a sandwich!

As a society, we need to debunk the myths that a slim body is always a healthy body; if you have an eating disorder like anorexia, it is often far from healthy. We need to learn about these conditions in depth, including the ugly truths, and change the way we perceive food and human bodies in general. If you think you are struggling with anorexia, I also urge you to be open to different solutions that will help you, not just survive it, but thrive in spite of it, every single day. After all, life's too short to weigh your cornflakes, so allow me to guide you through a journey to a new, empowered, and healthier chapter of your life by restoring your body and mind to where it once was, before anorexia reared her ugly head. I can't wait for you to be able to focus on the number of beautiful moments in your life rather than the numbers on your bathroom scales.

UNDERSTANDING ANOREXIA NERVOSA

When suffering from an eating disorder like anorexia nervosa, it can be difficult to look at yourself in a mirror. Your mind plays tricks on you despite your family and friends telling you that you are slim enough. Your eyes will show you something completely different, and you'll strive to lose even more weight. Your mind may also feel turbulent, overly emotional, and anxious, which can make you withdraw from your loved ones and negatively influence your eating patterns.

Even though I was feeling all of these things, I didn't even know what anorexia nervosa was while I was affected by it. I just knew that I felt and looked different from my peers and my former self. It was such a confusing and life-changing time for me, so instead of remaining ignorant, let's explore anorexia together, with the hope that this disorder becomes a little clearer, easier to talk about, and eventually, possible to recover from.

WHAT IS ANOREXIA NERVOSA?

The first and most important step on the journey towards healing is understanding what you are suffering from. According to the Cleveland Clinic, anorexia nervosa is a very serious eating disorder that affects approximately 1–2% of the American population and 0.3% of adolescents, so although serious, it is quite uncommon. People who have this disorder will limit the number of calories and types of food they eat, and it is usually accompanied by an intense fear of gaining weight. To relieve this fear, sufferers may exercise compulsively or intentionally vomit to purge any food that's already been eaten. This is not to be confused with bulimia, in which people eat an excessive amount of food in a short space of time and follow it by self-induced vomiting, misuse of laxatives or thyroid hormones, or continued fasting and exercise. People with bulimia are usually able to maintain their weight at an optimal level, whereas most people with anorexia have a body mass index (BMI) that is considered underweight.

However, anorexia can affect people of any age, gender, sex, race, sexual orientation, and economic status as well as people of all body weights, shapes, and sizes, so you can't necessarily tell if a person has anorexia just by their appearance. Furthermore, there is actually a sub-condition called atypical anorexia in which the patient displays all symptoms of anorexia nervosa apart from being underweight. The most important thing to understand about anorexia is that it is not a choice, but a health condition that takes over the mind and no matter how much food is put in front of a sufferer, it won't change their thought patterns or actions. Recovery requires time, patience, and often intervention because it is such a complex and overwhelming illness that can be triggered at any stage of life without the sufferer realizing they have it.

Triggers

Anorexia is often triggered by things that are out of our control. Social situations, lifestyle changes, genetics, or trauma can all make your brain act in ways that it's not supposed to, so it doesn't necessarily have anything to do with wanting to change the way you look.

For me, the trigger was having no sense of self. Everything was predetermined for me by my parents, from what my major would be at college to which school I would go to study, so I felt as though I had no control over my life and no allowance for independent thought. I also had a lot to live up to as my parents had great careers and my sister was already doing well in college. As well as this, I was considered the "it girl" who had a popular boyfriend, good grades, and lots of friends, so I started to behave as I thought I should in order to maintain this positive and successful image, but I never really felt happy or fulfilled by this. I felt like nobody understood or knew the real me. Nevertheless, I continued working on this image, but it made me feel lower and lower which significantly suppressed my appetite and I started to lose a lot of weight. I then began noticing that the more weight I lost, the more people would compliment me, and even at 92 pounds in my third year of high school, my peers would still say that I looked great. In hindsight, all of this positive reinforcement and attention I was getting led me to believe that my unhealthy lifestyle and weight loss was fine and became the beginnings of a vicious cycle which eventually put me on the path to anorexia.

So, how can you tell if you are suffering from anorexia or just have difficulty eating enough to maintain a healthy weight for other reasons? Well, there are physical, behavioral, and emotional/mental signs to look out for that are specific to this eating disorder.

Physical Signs

The most obvious and well-known physical sign of anorexia is having a very low body weight for your height, sex, and ethnic background. Low body weight is considered concerning when it drops below 15% of the expected weight for your demographic (Cleveland Clinic, n.d.). It's important to remember, however, that someone can have anorexia without being underweight and can also be underweight without having anorexia. Some people have high metabolisms, a naturally low level of body fat, or have other conditions such as an overactive thyroid that prevents them from putting on weight normally.

Extreme unhealthy weight loss can lead to health problems such as gallstones or arthritis and in severe cases, some people can sadly lose their lives. In addition to having low body weight, a sufferer will usually have physical symptoms that are related to starvation and malnutrition including dizziness or fainting, regularly feeling tired, a slow or irregular heartbeat, low blood pressure, and/or poor concentration. I remember being in class and feeling my heart start to race and pound heavily. I couldn't catch my breath and didn't understand why, but now I know that it is because our bodies need an ample amount of food to be able to function properly, so without this fuel, our bodily functions will start to behave strangely. Think of your body as a car. It might have shiny new rims and a state-of-the-art exterior design, but if there's not enough gas in the tank, it simply won't be able to do its job and get you around, no matter how good you or others think it looks.

A simplistic way to halt or reverse this physical sign of anorexia in its tracks is to eat more, but because of the complexity of this eating disorder, we all know that it can't be fixed that easily. So, my advice would be to take your time and try to do this, but also talk to those around you about how you are feeling, even if you experience signs of malnutrition just once. Don't ignore it like I did, because this is your body telling you that something isn't right and simply telling somebody might be the quickest way to get yourself out of the cycle of abusing your body.

Another sign of anorexia is having difficulty regulating your body temperature, so you may notice that you feel cold a lot of the time. I remember often cuddling up to my boyfriend at the time for warmth and he would never understand why I was shivering so much. This happens because having low body fat and poor circulation due to malnutrition means that you will struggle to maintain heat. One more sign is your period stopping or becoming irregular, which is known as amenorrhea. Primary amenorrhea is when you haven't had your first period by age 15 or within the first five years of puberty and secondary amenorrhea is when they stop for at least three months since starting. At your age, your periods may not be perfectly regular anyway, but it's something to look out for in the future.

Shortness of breath, bloating, abdominal pain, muscle weakness, poor wound healing, and frequent illness could also indicate starvation, but it's important to remember that to be considered as anorexia, these physical signs would need to be accompanied by psychological and behavioral signs too.

Behavioral Signs

If you or those close to you have noticed that your eating habits or routines have changed, this could be a behavioral sign of anorexia. For example, I started eating food in a specific order or rearranged the food on my plate to make it look as though I'd eaten more than I had. This sense of secrecy or deception could also show itself through wearing baggier clothing to hide your body because deep down, you know that what you are doing is not approved of by others. I personally also developed an unhealthy habit of weighing myself before and after showering, to see if I had lost weight during this short space of time.

Some people have a sudden change in their dietary preferences and intentionally eliminate certain food groups, such as carbohydrates or fats, from their diet completely. Although saturated fats are unhealthy, our bodies do need other fats and carbs to be able to carry out daily functions and give us energy, so removing them entirely can lead to all sorts of stamina or gut issues. Some sufferers may even refuse all food, or only eat enough to survive by constantly counting their calorie intake. For example, they might record everything they consume, including water, in a diary and add up the number of calories they eat each day in order to make sure they do not go over the bare minimum that is required to keep them alive.

When I was suffering, I would only drink a SlimFast shake in the morning and a bar for lunch, and the only real substantial meal I would have would be dinner that my mom cooked for me. This was not enough to sustain a healthy weight at all, so by the time I reached my second year of high school, my clothes were falling off me; I went from a size five or six in jeans in freshman year to a size zero as a senior and still, people rarely said anything about it.

As an attempt to curb these behaviors you could keep a diary or privatized blog of all the things you are doing or not doing that are having an effect on your weight and/or appearance. Seeing your behavior written down in this way will allow you to compare it to what is considered normal and healthy and help you see for yourself how detrimental these things can be to your overall well-being. This will hopefully make you stop, reevaluate, and change your actions before they become a habit. Sadly, this unusual dietary behavior, along with excessive exercise and constant comments about your body are all common among those with anorexia, and it suggests some mental health struggles too.

Mental and Emotional Signs

As we now know, anorexia is very much a disorder that affects the mind, so it's important to look out for the many mental and emotional signs. These often include irritability, depression, or obsession (i.e. having an obsessive interest in calories and dieting), and the need to be in control of what you do, wear, and eat all the time. The most prominent mental sign, however, is anxiety.

The National Institute of Mental Health estimates that approximately 47.9% of those with anorexia also struggle with an anxiety disorder, such as panic, phobias, and generalized anxiety disorder (GAD). This is because anorexia has very similar symptoms to anxiety, such as a hyperfixation on perfectionism, rigidity in daily living, and meticulousness (Rittenhouse, 2021), so they are usually treated alongside each other simultaneously.

Anxiety is a feeling of unease that leads to feeling worried or fearful. Everyone experiences it at some point in their lives, for example, just before you are about to sit for an exam or have a job interview. It's usually described as butterflies in your stomach or a rush of adrenaline through your body that usually makes you perform better, but if these feelings get out of hand or start to feel very intense, it can turn into panic, dizziness, sweaty palms, or even heart palpitations. If you are suffering from anorexia, you may start to feel this way at the idea of having to eat in front of people and over time you could even develop a genuine phobia of food itself, purely because it has the potential to make you put on weight. Anxiety might also kick in just before you weigh yourself or if your parents buy you new clothes as you worry how they will fit or draw attention to your body. Furthermore, when someone with anorexia does eat, a chemical reaction happens in their brain that triggers anxiety. There is a production of serotonin and dopamine hormones which increases levels of anxiety and tension, so eating will become linked to this negative feeling, thus making them not want to eat again.

People with anorexia may also struggle to regulate or even feel certain emotions entirely. When I was fighting this illness, I felt like I was on autopilot and would find it difficult to make close connections with people or feel genuine happiness. I had lost my emotional side to this disorder, and it made me feel numb and misunderstood. I now know that this is typical of anorexia, as many sufferers will put on a mask and try to act the same all the time with the hopes of evoking predictable and controllable behavioral patterns from others, but this is unrealistic and so emotionally unhealthy! For example, as a sufferer who is seen as a cool, calm, and quiet student at school and is constantly praised and celebrated for this, you would want to maintain this reaction from others so badly that any other natural emotions, such as frustration, excitement, or anger, will be suppressed and you'd eventually feel 'empty.' You would then stop eating because having intense emotional voids like this can lead to a lack of appetite or impaired eating controls. What's more, as an anorexia sufferer with a negative relationship with food, instead of wanting to fill these voids with food, as many non-sufferers do, you would find more comfort in not eating at all; emotional eating would not be an option.

This continuous suppression of emotions can either cause them to disappear completely or build up inside your mind, waiting to be released. Bottling up your emotions in this way can be very damaging not only to you, but to those around you too. For example, imagine that your mind is a car tire and the air is your emotions. The thick rubber of the tires will easily manage to contain a few pumps of air and carry the car on its journey. But as more air is pumped in with nowhere else to go, it will start to fill to capacity and the rubber will become stressed and tight. Its sides will bulge and struggle to maintain its normal shape and function, but it just about holds itself together for a few more journeys. If you then force more and more air into it, the next time it makes a journey, it may explode and cause you to crash. Emotional outbursts happen in a similar way and you may find yourself lashing out at the people you care about the most or having unbalanced reactions to everyday situations, so it's healthier to release your true and valid emotions steadily. It's okay not to be okay sometimes and letting how you feel out is often the best form of therapy.

Another sign that you may be suffering from anorexia is that you will try to regulate your emotions by focusing intensely on food, eating, weight, and shape so that you can avoid and distract yourself from any negative thoughts or feelings. For instance, you might purposefully spend hours counting and calculating the calories in your school lunch, so you don't have time to feel self-conscious about the way you look. On the surface this may sound like a great way to dodge sadness, but in reality, it isn't a healthy way to behave because you're not addressing and healing the true underlying emotion, but rather, masking it. It's like putting a bandaid on a huge wound; it might stop the bleeding for a short while, but it will never heal properly that way.

With your mental health in disarray, you may notice that you have difficulty getting to sleep or end up sleeping more than you need to. In fact, there has been found to be a clear link between eating disorders and sleeping issues which is why improving sleep patterns is just one of the ways people with this disorder get help. However, there are still some unknown factors as to why those with anorexia also suffer with poor sleep patterns since the processes surrounding sleep, nutrition, and mental health are very complex, making it difficult to get a definitive answer. It is also hard to know which factor triggers which, i.e., are you not getting enough sleep because you have anorexia, or do you have anorexia because you aren't getting enough sleep? It's a bit of a chicken and egg situation, but there are a few theories that researchers are looking into.

According to The Sleep Foundation, one theory is that because sleep plays a pivotal role in both emotional and physical health, disturbed sleep patterns and lower sleep quality creates a tumultuous anorexic mind and body. Another idea is that a lack of sleep prevents the brain from developing the areas responsible for planning, prioritizing, and controlling impulses, so a person who doesn't sleep enough is more likely to have difficulty with these processes, all of which are needed to keep eating disorders at bay. A further suggestion is that those who have inconsistent eating patterns and fail to consume nutrients such as B complex vitamins and omega–3, which are found in eggs, leafy greens, and meat (as do many who suffer from anorexia) can experience reduced sleep quality and daytime sleepiness because this malnutrition negatively affects the production of chemicals and hormones that control your sleep and wakefulness. Sleep is also directly involved in the normal production of hormones that regulate hunger and appetite, so disturbed sleep often disrupts this and results in unusual eating behavior.

Fortunately, there are ways in which you can take control and improve your sleep to potentially give yourself a fighting chance at battling this disorder. First, you need to commit to getting enough sleep for your body to function at optimal levels. Set an alarm that tells you to go to bed and when to wake up; the average teen should get approximately 8–10 hours of sleep per day (Suni, 2022). Next, you can upgrade your sleep hygiene.

This has nothing to do with the cleanliness of your sheets (although this will help), but everything to do with where and how you sleep. For example, you should make sure that your bedroom is designed in a way that is conducive to quality sleep by having a good quality mattress and bedding that makes your bed inviting and comfortable. You could use blackout drapes to block out sunlight, earplugs to block out sound, and a fan to keep the room at a cool temperature (approximately 65 degrees Fahrenheit). You should also try to prepare for bed in the same way each night, as we know that those who suffer from anorexia find comfort in routine, thus calming the mind and helping your body ease into a state of rest.

If you find that you sleep too much, setting an alarm on your phone and putting it across the room will ensure that you get out of bed to switch it off, which increases your chances of staying awake. You should then get washed, dressed, and out of your sleep area as soon as possible to avoid the temptation of your bed. You can also try to stay more motivated after school and on weekends by listening to music, learning a new skill, or talking to friends and family.

Your mental health should be your priority because it is the foundation of who you are, how you behave, and how you feel. Your mind is so powerful and, as much as it can get you into difficulty with disorders like this, you should remember that this state is temporary and you have the strength to get yourself out of it too. You can and will eventually improve the way you see yourself and your outlook on life in general.

SIGHT VS WEIGHT

Sadly, while suffering from anorexia, you may be triggered by or become obsessed with the way you look. The way you view your body will most likely be inaccurate, as one of the most common and significant indications that you have this disorder is if you are unable to realistically assess or recognize your body weight and shape i.e. you have a distorted self-image. For example, even if you are severely underweight, you will see somebody that is chubby or overweight in the mirror, and an inner voice will tell you to lose more weight. In simple terms, you have a 'sight' problem and not a weight problem, and this can be linked to another condition called body dysmorphia.

Body dysmorphia, or body dysmorphic disorder (BDD), often comes hand in hand with anorexia but it is not the same thing. It is a mental health condition where you spend an excessive amount of time solely worrying about your appearance, whereas people with anorexia experience eating problems as well. Many people with anorexia will also experience BDD, but not all people with BDD have anorexia, and sadly BDD affects 1 in 50 people in the United States (Haines, 2021).

Body dysmorphia can also make you compare your looks to others, go to extremes to conceal or change your perceived flaws, stare at yourself in the mirror for hours, or even avoid mirrors altogether. If you have BDD, these obsessions and false sense of identity will cause emotional distress and have a significant impact on your daily life, so it is not simply thinking that you are having a bad hair day. It can affect the way you see any area of your body, but common areas of anxiety include your skin, hair, nose, chin, lips, or genitals. In fact, eye-tracking studies have shown that if you have an eating disorder, your eye will focus on the parts of your body that you find least attractive for longer, which can make you more susceptible to BDD as well. You will hone in to the 'negative' attributes and become fixated on them so they seem a lot worse to you than they are in reality. For example, if you notice that your stomach slightly protrudes or is a little bit larger than you would like, you will focus on this area and then go on to believe that your entire body is too large. You'll then develop a need to change this, and as a young person, the only way this can be done is through diet and exercise.

It is argued that people who suffer from anorexia are also disproportionately reliant upon the feedback and opinion of others for reassurance (Rittenhouse, 2021). Wanting reassurance to a certain extent is normal. For example, girls will often ask each other how they look in an outfit or what others think about a new hairstyle, but for those suffering with eating disorders, this desire to know what other people think of them is constant and can actually lead to distress. Sufferers will relentlessly ask those around them for their opinion on how they look, if they are slim enough, or how pretty they are to make sure that there is nothing 'wrong' with them and with the hopes of being temporarily relieved by a positive response. But whether the answer is positive or negative, it is likely that a few moments later they will be worrying about it again and need to check their appearance once more.

If you find yourself engaging in this behavior, it is so important to try your best to break out of this cycle as soon as possible by consciously changing your thought pattern. A good way to do this is to look around at your friends and family. You will most probably notice that they are of different shapes and sizes. Does the way they look affect how much you love and care for them? Probably not. Or does their appearance determine how happy they deserve to be? Certainly not! So you should know that you also deserve care, love, compassion, and happiness too, regardless of the way you look; your appearance isn't really important in the grand scheme of things. What's really important is fulfilling your dreams, positively contributing to the world, and being a good person to yourself and others.

All of the signs and symptoms we've mentioned in this chapter are not easy to overcome on your own. If they were, then there would be no such thing as eating disorders, so don't put yourself down if you aren't able to curb these feelings straight away. Be patient and honest with yourself and do your best to eliminate any triggers around you that could be making your symptoms worse.

2

FAMILY DYNAMICS

Some eating disorders run in families, which suggests a possible genetic predisposition. Research has found that genetics are responsible for 40–50% of the risk of developing an eating disorder and, more specifically, a female with a mother or sister who has anorexia is 12 times more likely to develop the condition herself, compared to the general population (Eating Recovery Center, 2020). It is important, however, to know that there is more to anorexia than genetics and there is no 'fault' in your genes if you have an eating disorder.

So what role do your loved ones play in your disorder? Well, the dynamics within your family can play a part in how you experience and recover from anorexia, which was identified as far back as the late 19th century. It was found that many moms and dads of children with anorexia were often a hindrance to treatment as they showed higher signs of dysfunction, lower participation and organizational skills, and worse teamworking skills than those who didn't have a teen with an eating disorder (Mensi et al., 2020). These traits were all found to negatively affect recovery, so parents were often excluded from many aspects of the teen's medical treatment.

Today, however, these studies have been discredited because, in a lot of cases, families' actions and behavior do not cause any eating problems and genetics are nobody's fault, so you should not blame your family for giving you anorexia. In fact, according to the Oliver-Pyatt Center which looks after teens with eating disorders, it is now said that it is beneficial for your family, or those who are around you at home, to understand the disorder and be on board with any treatment that is recommended to you, as they will play a vital role in protecting and maintaining your recovery. But these early findings do suggest that we should be aware of the silent (and not so silent) negative triggers our families may still deliver that can make anorexia arise or worsen if you are particularly vulnerable to it.

PARENTS OR GUARDIANS

Although many parents and guardians usually act out of love for their children, nobody is perfect, and sometimes rigidity and over involvement in their child's life can have a negative effect on the child's relationship with themselves and their day-to-day functioning, including how they view food and manage eating. For example, imagine that your mom desperately wants you to achieve in sports. She may constantly monitor your wins and losses, nutrition, and fitness extremely closely in order to get the best out of you, but this can feel overbearing if it happens continuously. It can make you feel incapable of making your own decisions about what you do with your time and body, including what you eat and when. This can lead to you feeling fearful or unsure about food in general, eventually resulting in anorexia.

When I was growing up, I had a similar experience, in that my mom was involved in my school work, after-school activities, what I was doing with my friends on the weekend, and so on and so forth. However, my mom didn't really show any deeper interest in how I truly felt about school, my body, or my personal life goals. Neither of my parents ever brought up my weight or acknowledged the fact that my new clothes were becoming increasingly smaller in size to accommodate my shrinking waistline. I simply did what they said, how they said it, and rarely thought about what I wanted for myself. My life continued to be planned out in this way for many years and, in hindsight, I can see that we had become enmeshed, which means that I found it very difficult to function without her and even harder to develop my own identity. This made me withdraw significantly and I started to feel as though I didn't want to share my anxious feelings and concerns with anyone anymore. I felt as though my thoughts, emotions, and worries were invalid or unimportant and that my parents would see them as burdens, so I decided not to bother them with my additional pressures; after all, they had their own lives to deal with. But hiding my emotions for such a long time in this unhealthy way and not knowing who I was eventually manifested itself into low mood and then anorexia. Sadly, later on when I did find the courage to open up to my parents about my eating and mental health struggles, my feelings were pushed aside as trivial, with comments such as "get over it," "you're being too sensitive," or "you're making too big a deal out of it." This was so disheartening and made me go into my shell once again.

If you've heard these kinds of comments from your parents too, it could be because they are of a generation that sees eating disorders as a sign of vanity with a sole focus on becoming thin, so they may consider it fickle or a form of attention seeking.

They probably have an outdated or simplistic view of the condition with some calling it a fashion statement, lifestyle choice, or just a teenage phase. But in reality, nobody chooses to be anorexic and the condition can feel terrifyingly ruthless, with attention being the last thing you want at times! So, in order to stop this misconception about anorexia in its tracks, we need to educate older generations about it. There are social networks, podcasts, TV shows, articles, and even events out there that can help them understand what it is you are going through, so even if you can't find the words, you can point them in the direction of reliable information. This will hopefully end the stigma and misunderstanding, and instead, start the conversation.

The fact that my parents were very busy and out of the house a lot meant that I was regularly on my own with nobody to talk to. This gave my mind time to wonder and overthink, and my anorexia symptoms had the space to thrive; I was able to eat as little as I wanted with no questions or challenges. Being alone at home so much also made me feel isolated and lonely despite having an active social life. But how can this be? Well, it's because our sense of loneliness comes from within. Some people can be by themselves and feel very content, whereas others can be surrounded by people and still feel lonely because they don't feel understood or cared for by those people. This is why spending quality time with your parents or guardians is so valuable, whether you talk or not. Just being around them often will make you feel more comfortable in their presence and will give them a chance to pick up on any signs that something isn't quite right with your behavior or body. This could then prompt them to ask that short, yet powerful question: "Are you okay?" Those three words will feel like a huge weight has been lifted from your shoulders and be the catalyst to the beginning of your healing journey, but you all need to be present for this to happen; you don't have to have the answer, just do your best to ask for and make space for the opportunity to discuss.

Now, I acknowledge that having quality time with your parents may not be a possibility for you if you live in an unstable environment or are no longer in their care and, unfortunately, this lack of or poor parental presence can be a trigger in itself. It has been found that teens who are living in dysfunctional families, moving between separated parent's homes, or are in foster care are more likely to be affected by anorexia and other eating disorders than their peers who live in more settled environments (Center for Discovery, 2019). This is because of a combination of factors such as an increased likelihood to be exposed to inconsistent and conflicting rules, uncertain living or sleeping arrangements, arguing, and sadly even, abuse, which can all be very disconcerting, emotionally damaging, and disruptive for teens who need routine and can cause young minds to react in ways that are conducive to anorexia development.

FATHER FIGURES

If you live with your dad or father figure, it is normal for them to have a male perspective of the female teen body and mind, so they may not appreciate the complexities of how your brain works, which can sometimes lead to dismissal or denial of eating disorders like anorexia. Some men believe that girls are meant to be very slim, so may not consider drastic weight loss as a problem and, as they tend to be more tough-minded and emotionally stable on average (Kaufman, 2019), they are more likely to wonder what all your 'fuss' is about. Research also shows that men tend to use more assertive speech and are more likely to interrupt people when they speak as a dominant form of behavior, so young teens may even find it intimidating talking to male figures about something as personal as an eating disorder. Of course, there are many dads who don't display these traits, but if yours does, I understand that you may feel like you are in a difficult situation.

There isn't much focus on father-daughter relationships when it comes to studying eating disorders and their treatments, but it has been found that many girls who suffer from anorexia and attend therapy will describe their fathers as 'absent' or 'busy,' suggesting that their relationship is poor. Their father's absence and silence was then interpreted as uncaring, but this is often actually a sign of helplessness. Many men feel as though they shouldn't express this feeling due to societal pressures of what it means to be a man, so they'd rather take a step back. They may also not know how to support you, so avoid you with the hopes that your problems may disappear or that you "grow out of it." This was true for me, as my dad was largely absent due to work, but when he was around, instead of taking on the traditional role of protector, he would make jokes about the way I looked as I started to lose weight, calling me a "bone rack." This was very hurtful, but I don't think he even realized the impact these words can have on a young girl and, even if the comments aren't directed at us in particular, we do pick up on misogynistic comments or jokes said to our moms or about females in general. For example, a therapist at Center for Change said that she had a young client who told her that her dad would often criticize her mom for being fat, even though she wasn't, and told her to watch what she ate. Another client even indicated that her father agreed to pay her mum to lose weight so that she would be more attractive to him. Being exposed to these words and actions can make young female sufferers question what it means to be and look like an attractive woman, and increase their desire to change the way they look through diet and exercise to an unhealthy extent. They may start thinking "If my dad doesn't love my mom's body as it is, maybe he doesn't love me," which can be a very sad and triggering moment.

Again, making jokes or rough play could be his way of attempting to understand you better and get closer to you if he feels as though he is struggling to find a way in. It could also be a way for him to avoid or divert his own feelings of worry or concern for you. Now, this doesn't excuse the fact that his words or actions hurt your feelings, but it does show how important it is to honestly express what feels good and bad to you in the moment if you can in order to stop them from sparking depressive thoughts. Most of the time, good dads will listen and change their behavior if they know it is damaging.

As females, on average we tend to be more polite, sensitive, and compassionate, which can be detrimental to us when it comes to coping with conditions like anorexia. This can be seen in the relationship we have with our fathers and food. Fathers are traditionally seen as the providers of food and money, and sometimes this view can be made clear by how they are at the dinner table. Some sufferers have experienced their fathers requesting that they finish their food even if they don't want to because if they don't, it is deemed disrespectful, i.e. "If you love and respect me, you will eat the food I have provided for you." This can make mealtimes very stressful and, as a compassionate and vulnerable girl not wanting to disappoint the "head of the home," they do so, but feel terrible about it afterwards, thus building a negative relationship with their father and food.

With these situations in mind, I urge you to be brave and find your voice. Teens can be just as assertive and confident as men, so do your best to have an open conversation with the father in your life, or if it's not possible, make sure that you tell somebody about the impact his actions are having on your mental and physical health as soon as you can.

EXTENDED FAMILY

Many of us have large extended families including cousins, aunts, uncles, and more, so you would think that this provides plenty of opportunity to find and engage with someone you can relate to and express your concerns about your condition. However, when you suffer from anorexia, having a big family can actually make you feel more isolated. This is because, no matter what culture you are from, food is a universal way of bringing people together. Whether it be birthday parties, dinners, barbecues, weddings, or restaurants, so many of us use food to socialize, so if you have anxiety around it, it is likely that these events are your worst nightmare and you will do your best to avoid them. This often worsens feelings of disconnection from your family and even results in social withdrawal syndrome where you may make up excuses for not attending such gatherings because deep down, you don't want the disapproving comments or stares when you refuse food.

Research has also found that those with eating disorders have low trust in others (Cleveland Clinic, n.d.), so being around lots of extended family members you don't know very well can feel awkward and stressful. They may stare at you and ask personal questions about the way you look or eat and you may not trust them enough to want to answer. This could then trigger feelings of shame or guilt, leading to a loss of appetite and worse eating habits. If you attend a function where this happens to you, I believe that it is best to move away from these people while respectfully but honestly saying that you don't want to talk about your appearance. Ultimately, as long as you are comfortable in what you are wearing and are trying to eat more in your own time, you shouldn't have to prove or explain anything to anyone you don't trust.

Older family members may also have outdated gender expectations and believe that young girls should look a certain way. This can lead to them constantly telling you that you look 'wrong' in their eyes. For example, they may tease you about the fact you wear baggy clothes, lack youthful curves, or have thinner hair than your siblings, and therefore conclude that you "look like a boy" instead of recognizing that these are signs of something troubling you and offering support. As a young girl, this can be hurtful and nobody wants to be around hypercritical people like this, especially if you suffer from low self-esteem, so it's little wonder gatherings like this are unappealing to those suffering from anorexia. In my experience, the older generation may even go as far as recognizing a potential eating disorder in someone but still do nothing about it as not to acknowledge a 'weakness' in the family. I remember when I was younger, my grandmother asked my sister if I had an eating disorder after noticing the changes in my appearance. My sister said no, but when I entered the room, there my grandmother was with a tape measure to measure me. My body was tiny and, when I look back on it, my waist was shockingly small, so the measurements must have confirmed that I wasn't well, but from that day on, nothing further was ever said about it.

These strains on our relationships with our extended family can affect our view of cross-generational alliances and make it more difficult for sufferers to seek professional help because a lot of the time, the therapists who deal with eating disorders will be of an older age. But remember, this strain and friction is due to ignorance on your family's part and professionals will never judge, make fun of, or ignore you.

SIBLINGS

If you have any brothers or sisters, you will know that it's totally normal to have some form of conflict or friction between you every now and then, even if your relationship is positive overall. When you add an eating disorder to the mix, however, your relationship may unfortunately start to feel more tense than normal and even alter how they treat and view you.

If you have older siblings, you might find that they start treating you like a doll. They may already be protective of you, but because you are now more vulnerable, the protective instinct could increase tenfold. This can be a good thing if you feel as though you can use them as a support or listening ear, but some may find this treatment overbearing or babying, especially if they start talking for you or taking on parental roles. Although anorexia is ultimately a mental health condition, it doesn't generally affect cognitive ability, so having a sibling treat you in this way wouldn't be the nicest feeling. Furthermore, if your siblings are younger and they do this, it could leave you feeling guilty for being a burden or as though you are not doing your 'job' as an older sister.

In some cases, your sibling will not voluntarily take on the role of your carer, but your parents might say things like "look after your sister" or "your sister needs you to help her" and as a result, additional responsibilities will fall on their shoulders. This can unfortunately lead to resentment, frustration, or jealousy because of the treatment and attention you are getting as the 'sufferer' in the family. A lot of your sibling's time may be taken up by checking on you, accompanying you to appointments, or encouraging you to feel better, so they might start to wonder if anyone cares about how they feel or what they want to do anymore. Sometimes, this lack of attention leads to siblings going "off the rails" as a form of rebellion or because parents are distracted and cannot offer the support, guidance, and discipline they should be giving. The usual quality time you would have as a family may also be disrupted because of your care needs and the financial burden of treatment may mean that siblings are no longer allowed to have certain things. But don't worry, none of this will be directly your fault, and if they are old and wise enough to recognize that you have an illness and are not needing extra support out of choice, they are likely to understand why you need them to be a little compassionate and the sibling love will surely kick back in.

Unfortunately, feelings of jealousy can work both ways and you could potentially become jealous of siblings who aren't suffering in the way you are. You may begin to envy the freedom, control, and confidence they have and, despite your best efforts to heal, wonder why you've been affected by anorexia and not them. This is a completely normal emotion in these circumstances, but it should be curbed because it is nobody's fault that you have this disorder. You are still the talented, smart, and loved member of the family you've always been, with your own worth, so if you focus on these positive aspects rather than the negative aspects of your life, you will see that you both have qualities to be thankful for.

If your siblings don't fully understand anorexia, it can make your interactions with them a little strained because you are likely to be more sensitive to comments about your appearance. You may have brushed off general teasing or name-calling before your diagnosis, but because you now have a heightened sense of discomfort and are already suffering mentally, you'll probably take these jibes more seriously. In addition to this, siblings could start to make positive remarks about how tiny your clothes are and or how slim your body is because of their failure to understand how unhealthy anorexia is or because of their awareness of how society values small bodies. For example, my sister would make comments about how thin I was as if it was a positive attribute and react to my small clothes as if she was jealous that I could fit into them. Whatever the circumstance, ignorance and dismissal like this can only be cured by education, so the more you and your parents understand anorexia, the easier it will be to talk coherently to your siblings about the struggles you are facing, and why certain comments and actions are unhelpful for your healing.

It is recommended by Feast Ed that siblings of those affected by anorexia are provided with age-appropriate information as soon as a diagnosis is given. It should include the symptoms as well as the proposed treatment so that they are prepared for what the journey through anorexia entails. Being honest and realistic with them will stop you from minimizing the seriousness of eating disorders and help them understand why such immediate care needs to be taken. Your parents should also create and enforce firm rules around triggering behaviors in order to protect your sensitivity around food, weight, exercise, and body image, and this should nip any unhelpful comments in the bud. This education can make them feel closer to you, value your presence more, improve their own body image, become more mature, and make them aware of their own behaviors, just in case they start to show any early signs of anorexia too. They may even become an advocate to help others recover from eating disorders and remove the stigma.

As we can see, there may be a need to change your family dynamics in order to heal properly in an active and united way. The main thing to remember is that your family isn't against you. They ultimately care about your well-being and they may wish they had a better connection with you. In fact, many family members often say that they have sadly 'lost' their loved one to an eating disorder even if they are still around because sufferers usually withdraw so much (Center for Discovery, 2019). So I implore you to seek help, not only for your sake, but for your family's well-being too.

3

FRIENDSHIPS

During adolescence, friends often feel like the next best thing to family members, being described as "the family you choose." We see teen movies, television shows, and social media posts that show images of best friends all living happy and fun lives, but in the reality of an anorexia sufferer, this representation of teen life can feel a little unrelatable. This is because eating disorders dominate so much of our lives that building healthy friendships becomes very difficult and the friends we already have may unintentionally trigger us or be unhelpful when it comes to our healing process. So, let's explore how and why this happens with the hopes of developing wholesome and more beneficial friendships.

BORN TO BE DIFFERENT?

Teenage life comes with its highs, lows, and all that's in between. For most teenagers, the 'highs' usually include having more independence, dating, and experimenting with fashion and makeup. A common teenage 'low,' however, is the desire to fit in with your friends and fellow students. This longing to be like everyone else is considered as a 'low' because it can trigger a lot of anxiety and self-esteem issues during a time when you are still discovering who you are, learning what you like and dislike, and frantically navigating your way through hormonal changes. If this desire to blend in becomes a regular habit, it can lead to the manifestation of anorexia and here's why.

As you go through school, you might start to notice that you have a different body shape to your friends and other girls around you. You might be a little curvier or taller than them and these differences are completely normal as every girl's body changes at different times and rates, and even after puberty, our bodies will naturally continue to look different from each other. Sadly, insecurities and social standards around what girls 'should' look like at your age could lead you down the dangerous road of comparison. For example, you may notice that a lot of your friends are slender and athletic looking, so you start thinking that something is wrong with you because your body isn't the same. Understandably, nobody wants to feel like the oddball at school and there is an innate desire to be considered 'normal' at this age so that you don't get picked on. However, when you start to fixate on body differences and compare yourself to others while desperately trying to change your shape by restricting your diet on a regular basis, this can be a sign of something more serious like anorexia. You might do things like taking note of your friends' dress sizes and lunch meals and make it your goal to be smaller or eat less than them everyday, which is an unhealthy competitive relationship with food and body image associated with anorexia.

Social currency also needs to be considered here because at school, how popular you are is often misinterpreted as how valuable you are i.e. the more friends you have, the more you are worth as a person. Therefore, if you notice that you look different to some of the more popular girls in school, you might then start to think that you are worthless and decide to change yourself through starvation and unhealthy eating patterns. This need to change the way you look in order to be considered worthy of friendship could sadly drive you towards this dangerous eating disorder. So instead, I encourage you to remember that every healthy body type is beautiful, unique, and desirable in its own way, and as you get older, you will realize that popularity in the real world is not, in fact, based on the way you look but who you are on the inside. You can be tall or short, curvy or slim; as long as you are healthy and happy, you will find your tribe. The circle of friends you are meant to have will gravitate towards you and love you for your personality and common interests, not because of how you look, so why strive to look like others when you were born to be the unique and amazing person you already are?

Sometimes, the pressure to change your appearance will come from external sources at school, such as bullies, who have been found to be significant triggers for anorexia. Shockingly, 77% of school students report being a victim of bullying (Pipitone, n.d.), so experiencing this alongside other vulnerabilities can become a 'perfect storm' for eating disorder development; 65% of people with eating disorders say bullying contributed to their condition (National Eating Disorders Association, n.d.). Being bullied because of your body image will increase anxiety and depression, encourage withdrawal, and evoke feelings of worthlessness, so if you are particularly vulnerable, you might seek relief by not eating as an attempt to change your appearance and look less like a target. The bullies may not hurt you physically, but the words they use can be just as, if not more, hurtful; the phrase "sticks and stones may break my bones, but words can never hurt me" couldn't be any less true in this case, so you should tell a teacher or trustworthy friends as soon as your feel uncomfortable. You could also try some positive self-talk, also known as affirmations, to counterbalance the negative words you are hearing from others. For example, take a few minutes each day to tell yourself that you are strong, confident, and loved, because it's true!

DISTANT FRIENDS

If you are already in the grips of anorexia and are part of an established friendship group of healthy peers, it is likely that you look and behave differently to them, but unfortunately not in a healthy way. You might be a lot slimmer than them, struggle in social situations around food in ways they don't, and may not have gone through puberty in the way they have, all because of this dangerous disorder. Much like with your family, instead of risking questions from your friends about these differences, you might find yourself purposefully spending less and less time with them, leaving you feeling isolated. Some close friends may pick up on this distance as a cry for help and try to intervene, but others could be totally oblivious to your struggles or not see it as a serious problem. For me, I felt as though my friends and I were constantly ignoring the elephant in the room because in our free time, we went out to movies, small dinners, and held parties for each other. We discussed classes, projects, college applications, and potential schools; I never brought up how I felt and they never mentioned anything about my physical appearance. Because of this, after a while, I could feel myself drifting away from them emotionally and physically and began to think that how I was treating my body was fine. I even remember a time when we had a pool party and one of my friends mentioned they could see my ribs when I breathed in and out, however, we quickly changed the subject to something superficial and life went on.

As an adult, I can see that their remarks and my silence was probably a mixture of their lack of knowledge on eating disorders, the fact that they had their own teenage concerns, and my own insecurities. I also now understand that they were making small remarks here and there to acknowledge that something wasn't right but weren't quite sure how to address it. Unfortunately, this perfect storm made me feel even more alone, especially in social situations.

Other accounts show that teens with anorexia will start distancing themselves from their peers purposely because they either feel ashamed of their disorder, want to prevent more people fussing over them outside of the home, or even fear that their friends might stop them from carrying out their unhealthy eating rituals. By skipping class or dropping out of social gatherings on the weekends, sufferers can also hide the extent of the changes to their bodies and avoid the questions that may follow. When sufferers do see their friends at school, they might further the disconnect by lying about why they're not eating or completely refuse to talk about their weight loss, and this is often because of trust issues.

Trust is a huge part of any friendship. According to the One Love Foundation, it is one of the most important requirements for developing any healthy relationship, so you should have confidence in your friends' trustworthiness and feel as though you can count on them when you need them most. A good friend will also treat what you tell them with confidentiality and respect but, as we know, when suffering from anorexia, you could start to doubt these qualities because of the mental turmoil you are in. You might start to worry that if you open up to your friends about your disorder, they will not keep it a secret and instead spread that fact around school, so you decide to not tell anyone, thus pushing your friends away. Another pillar of friendship is honesty, so lying or concealing the truth about your disorder can make friendships feel very superficial and cause a lot of hurt. So, in order to avoid lying anymore, you might prefer to distance yourself from friends even more.

If you do decide to tell your friends about your eating disorder, how your friends react might determine how you build friendships in the future. For example, if you muster up the courage to open up and they laugh or dismiss what you tell them, you might vow not to tell any other friends and feel trapped in secrecy. This can lead to you feeling unable to build meaningful connections with people making life quite lonely. However, if you tell them and they gather round to support, listen, and understand you, you are more likely to feel empowered and confident to tell others in the future and get the treatment you deserve. With this in mind, think carefully about who you tell and when so that you hopefully have a smooth and positive experience, but regardless of how your friends react, taking this step shows a high level of courage and it is one move closer to recovery.

Because of all of these difficulties making and maintaining real-life friends, those suffering from anorexia may start to be drawn to virtual friends on platforms such as Instagram, TikTok, or Facebook. This is fine if you are looking for a little distraction from time to time, but these social media apps all come with many flaws and triggers for those with anorexia, so be careful how you use them and how much time you spend on them.

SOCIAL MEDIA

If you are a teen with a cell phone and regular internet connection, you are probably one of the millions of people across the world who use social media. Social media has been proven to be a huge part of teenage life in particular, with 97% of 13–17 year olds using it regularly (Mayo Clinic, 2022), despite its age restrictions. Most teenagers use it for positive things such as communicating with friends and family and building connections with people outside of their immediate circle. Others use it as a tool for inspiration for creative projects or simply as a source of entertainment. However, we should all be aware that there are some negative aspects hidden in these digital squares of perfection that could make you feel low, especially if you have, or are vulnerable to, eating disorders.

Despite social media being sold to us as a great way to make friends, using it a lot can be very disruptive to your daily life and a 2019 study even showed that teens who spend more than three hours per day using it are at a higher risk of mental health problems such as depression and anxiety. Users are also more susceptible to poor general well-being and sleep deprivation, all of which can trigger the development of anorexia (Mayo Clinic, 2022). Worryingly, Dove's latest research showed that young people spend an average of five hours on social media (Mayo Clinic, 2022), so, if you decide to use it to form or maintain friendships, be mindful of how long you use it for. It is also important to be aware that they have the potential to expose you to things like cyberbullying and rumor spreading, which is the complete opposite of what you are trying to achieve.

Cyberbullying often takes the form of sending or sharing hurtful content online as a way of embarrassing or threatening others and according to Security.org, 21% of children have experienced it. It was particularly prevalent between January and July 2020 during the COVID-19 lockdown because there was an increase in social media use, with 44% of all internet users in the United States saying that they had experienced online harassment during this time (Security.org, 2022). This type of bullying is damaging because it is hard to escape from. Before the creation of social media, once you left the school grounds, you had more of a chance of avoiding name-calling or teasing, but now, even in the comfort of your own home, bullies have a way of reaching you, so it can feel very intense and relentless. This can drive you deeper into your eating disorder, so if you ever feel bullied, I urge you to delete your accounts as soon as you can and focus on nurturing real friendships with those you know and trust.

Another reason social media may not be a great place to build friendships if you suffer from anorexia is because when online, you are likely to be bombarded with countless images of beautiful, slim, and happy friends and influencers who seem to be living near perfect lives. These snapshots can literally influence you to change the way you look and live in unhealthy ways with the hopes of achieving the same popularity and success they seem to have. You might start to spend too much of your pocket money on clothes or accessories to imitate their lifestyle, feel the need to use filters extensively to look like them, or even try to lose an excessive amount of weight to change your body, which is a gateway to many eating disorders. As we know, this comparison and desire to look like others does happen in real life too, but the dangerous difference is that when viewing people on apps like Facebook and Instagram, you can't necessarily tell if what you are seeing is real or if it has been edited to look as 'perfect' as it does. Unfortunately, most of the time, these images which are presented as reality have indeed been edited as found in a Forbes study. It revealed that editing apps such as FaceTune, which has the capability to slim people's faces and bodies in photos, had a 20% increase in its usage at the beginning of 2020 and continues to have over one million edited images exported daily (Haines, 2021). Settings like the "Enhance" feature on TikTok and the "Touch up my appearance feature" on Zoom, which make people's skin look flawless in videos, have also become extremely popular, and 42% of girls admit to using filters every day. Another study showed that 77%

of girls reported to change or hide at least one part of their body before posting online and 80% of girls have used an app to change their appearance before the age of 13 (Haines, 2021). This suggests that a lot of what we are seeing online is actually unrealistic, unattainable, and false representation, so your natural healthy body and face is actually far more 'normal' than you may think!

Before the likes of Instagram and TikTok existed, teens would only really compare themselves to their real life friends who looked very much like them or images of supermodels or celebrities on TV or in magazines. Teens knew that these models were far detached from their reality. Flawless skin and tall, slender bodies were almost seen as 'superhuman,' so it didn't matter that they looked different or seemed to have 'better' bodies; it was to be expected of the models, but not the average teen. Now, however, with easy access to airbrushing and filters on social media, all of your peers seem to look like these once inaccessible models, so you might start to think that this is the 'normal' way to look, which can lead you to a warped sense of what is attractive and healthy for the female body. Furthermore, if you decide to use online filters on yourself, when you look into a real mirror, you might start to feel uglier or fatter which plays right into the hands of body dysmorphia and, potentially, anorexia.

In a 2021 Forbes interview, Dr. Egger said that the use of Instagram and Snapchat has taken body dysmorphia and eating disorders to a whole new level. This is because disorders like anorexia are competitive in the sense that a sufferer's mind can make them believe that they should strive to be smaller or lighter than their peers or former selves in order to feel good or be accepted by others, regardless of the health implications. This competition is exaggerated on social media because of the 'likes' system. For example, as a sufferer, you might notice that a selfie you posted has 50 likes from your friends. This will feel great because each 'like' will seem like peer validation and provide a hit of dopamine (the happy hormone), so you continue to take photos of yourself and post them. One day however, you might come across an image of a girl who is a bit slimmer than you and see that she has 100 likes for her photo. Your mind might then tell you that she is getting more positive attention than you because of her lower weight which will encourage you to lose weight, with the hopes of receiving more 'likes' than her next time. This cycle can continue and you could get sucked into what Dr. Jasmine Fardouly from the Department of Psychology at Macquarie University calls an "envy spiral" until you make yourself very ill. A therapist at the Magnolia Creek Center has even had anorexia patients use the number of Instagram likes to determine whether they were going to eat that day or not, so this is a sad yet very real and serious issue.

Even if you plan on just using these platforms to make friends, you might come across thousands of posts about weight loss, workout routines, and dieting on social media because a lot of people use these platforms as motivation to lose weight or get in shape. As a teenager who is still developing and is suffering from anorexia, this can be a serious trigger, so try to avoid these types of posts by being careful with who you decide to follow and don't be afraid to unfollow any profile that makes you feel bad. Also try to limit the time spent on them by downloading apps that stop you using them for more than three hours per day.

Fortunately, social media is changing for the better, especially for those who suffer from eating disorders and body dysmorphia. In 2019 ,Instagram banned certain filters that alter your appearance in unhealthy ways and TikTok now indicates when a filter has been used. Young people are also far more open about the way they look without makeup and are embracing their natural bodies, whatever the size. Hashtags such as #NEDAselfie have even been created to encourage people to post unfiltered selfies with a caption about what makes them feel confident in their own natural skin (Magnolia Creek Center, 2019). This will help you remember that no matter what you look like, you have value and should feel positive about both the parts you deem as positives and the parts of your body you consider as 'flaws'–after all, every human on earth has flaws behind the filters, including your friends.

TRUE FRIENDS

Genuine friendship and authentic connections with people can be so beneficial to your experience of and recovery from anorexia. Being surrounded by supportive, kind, and patient friends of a similar age can really make all the difference because they will be able to relate to other teen pressures that could be linked to your eating disorder and promise not to do things that induce triggers. They will let you know that they are there for you, will try not to get angry or frustrated if you struggle to change your habits and won't make assumptions about why you've been affected by anorexia. That way, you can just focus on healing from the inside out.

In some treatment centers, group therapy is an option, so having your friends there at that stage could also be helpful. In fact, cognitive dissonance-based interventions (CDIs) where sufferers would participate in group discussions, roleplays, writing, and self-affirmation exercises with friends have been used to prevent eating disorders by inspiring harmony between the mind and the body. In the session you would criticize the "thin-ideal" with the hopes of recognizing your unhealthy behavior before it develops into something more serious. A study of school children ages 14–18 in the UK, showed that these types of interventions made sufferers feel a sense of belonging and find it easier to open up to their friends going forward. They then managed to transition to a more positive sense of body image quicker than those who didn't have the support of their friends. This could be because peer intervention will feel more personal and you will be held accountable beyond the session, so many professionals believe this type of CDI should be included in anorexia prevention and treatment as standard (Jarman et al., 2021).

Developing friendships within treatment spaces can also improve recovery (Walden Behavioural Care, n.d.) but be careful because it can come with some risks. The good thing about making friends who are also sufferers is that you can bond over a shared experience, which is rare to find. You'll have a stronger sense of understanding than your other friends, making it easier for you to empathize with each other and encourage each other to heal in a specialized environment. On the other hand, you might relate so much that you end up being enmeshed with each other and, just as you can feel positive when they feel positive, you can also feel low when they do and sink further into the disorder together. In this case, it's worth remembering that you are on your own journey and don't need to follow in the footsteps of those around you. Always make time for yourself and speak to your carers about any concerns.

True friends will be there for you from start to finish and remember that:

The greatest healing therapy is friendship and love. –Hubert H. Humphrey, Jr.

4

SIGNIFICANT OTHERS

As a teenager, you might have already reached the exciting milestone of your first date. Whether you suffer from an eating disorder or not, dating can feel like a daunting and sometimes awkward rite of passage, but when you do find that special someone, it can feel amazing. They'll give you butterflies in your tummy and giddy smiles and life will seem perfect. However, if you have anorexia, worry and doubt might start creeping back into your mind as you realize that at some point, you might have to have "the talk."

In this case, "the talk" refers to discussing your mental health and eating disorder with your significant other, which is understandably a conversation you'd rather not have. Similarly to platonic friends, you might feel as though your partner won't understand you or will judge you and walk away, and because heartbreak can feel so scary, you might even have a strong urge to just keep it to yourself. Some sufferers may even steer clear of relationships completely in order to avoid having to tell anyone.

All of these feelings are completely natural because, as humans, we usually want companionship, so we wouldn't want to do or say anything that could potentially reduce our chances of having it. However, if you are currently dating, it is worth looking at your relationship and seeing if there are any triggers, signs, or challenges that are detrimental to your health or are not conducive to your anorexia recovery. These signs might mean that you need to take a break from the relationship, regardless of how much you like them, or be brave enough to start the conversation so that you can get through it together.

ROMANTIC CHALLENGES

Romantic relationships require certain qualities like honesty, intimacy, and vulnerability from both partners in order to be successful and healthy. Unfortunately, having an eating disorder makes these qualities difficult to express which can be hard for partners to understand and lead to frustration. But if you identify these challenges early, you can take steps to repair those cracks and develop an even more meaningful connection.

Honesty

Honesty might be difficult to achieve in a relationship if you are an anorexia sufferer because you will probably find it hard to open up to your partner about having the condition. This can make you feel like you are hiding a dirty secret, which will eventually put a strain on any relationship. Eating disorders also thrive on secrecy and isolation, so sufferers will often 'protect' their eating rituals by keeping them to themselves or lying about them. For example, you might tell your partner that you've already eaten if they offer you dinner, even though you know you haven't really had any food all day or you might tell them you just have the flu if you start shivering from malnutrition. These may seem like small lies to you, but they could build up and make it difficult for you to keep track of what you've said. Your partner may then pick up on this and cause them to distrust you.

On the other hand, you might start to distrust your partner and their intentions because anorexia will try to force you away from anyone who threatens your perceived control of your body. You might start to think of your partner as a liar or a threat when they try to tell you how beautiful you are, persuade you to eat, or discourage you from overexercising, when in reality they are just trying to help.

Intimacy

Being intimate includes hugging, holding hands, and having deep and meaningful conversations about your feelings and desires. This level of intimacy might be difficult for you because people suffering from anorexia often feel self-conscious about their body or looks in general. My ex-boyfriend would make comments about the way I looked, saying that I was so skinny that he could feel my hip bones and rib cage when we embraced. He would say that I was "big-boned" and this made me worry about being too curvy and too slim at the same time, so I often stopped him from hugging me. These comments lowered my self-esteem even more and although he might have meant it as a joke, it made me not want to be intimate with him anymore. If you have experienced something similar, you have probably noticed that it has caused some tension in your relationship, but it's okay; you should never allow anyone to touch you if you feel uncomfortable in any way. Any reason you have to withhold intimacy is completely valid, whether you are in a relationship with them or not, because you are the only one with ownership of your body. You should try not to succumb to any pressure, but instead use this as an opportunity to work out why you are afraid of intimacy and take as long as you need to understand yourself. It could be that you are indeed self-conscious about the way you look, but it could also be the fact that you are so preoccupied with what food you've eaten or not eaten and how much you weigh that any form of intimacy doesn't even cross your mind. Once you address the reason, you can start to work on moving towards intimacy when you are completely ready.

Vulnerability

When suffering from anorexia, many girls also feel the need to be in control of everything, from the food they eat to the clothes they wear and the activities they take part in. When in a relationship, however, there needs to be a sense of compromise which requires both partners to let their guard down a little and listen to the other person's needs. This can be a huge hurdle for sufferers to get over as it takes vulnerability. Ideally, you'd relinquish a little control to allow your partner to plan dates, try new adventures, and simply enjoy your teen years together, but a lot of the time, sufferers find this too much to bear and sadly the relationship can begin to feel stale and one-sided.

Your relationship might also feel strained if your lack of vulnerability makes it difficult for you to express your full range of emotions or true personality. For example, when you first met, your partner may have initially been attracted to you because you exuded confidence. You may have put yourself across as a loud, bubbly, and seemingly extroverted girl, but this could have just been a mask you used to hide your true personality and anorexia symptoms. In reality, you might be shy, self-conscious, and introverted, but feel pressured to maintain this self-assured energy whenever you are with them, even if you don't really feel confident inside. After a while, this could make you feel as though you are unable to be your vulnerable and true self and your inner chaos will be suppressed until you can't take it anymore. This is very unhealthy for the relationship because your partner might start to think they don't know the real you and can lead to further anxiety and depression, or even arguments. So try your best to let your real self shine through your diagnosis because being vulnerable allows healing and a deeper, more meaningful connection.

Couple Goals

We've all seen images of perfect couples on social media or the perfect prom king and queen at school, with people making comments like "They look so good together" or "They are #couplegoals." A lot of the time this is purely based on their outward appearance, so some partners who enjoy this kind of attention may just focus on how you look together rather than how you feel together. Sadly, these superficial values aren't a very strong foundation for long-lasting relationships and it can add pressure on you to look the same way you did when you first met. You might even be fearful of no longer being your partner's 'type' if you change the way you look in any way. You might start to panic over putting on a few pounds and worry that you won't be deemed the "hot couple" anymore. Your partner might even make suggestions to you about how you should look to maintain the 'right' image. This can be not only disheartening as it suggests that the way you look isn't good enough, but also triggering as you could then find yourself in a vicious circle of trying to look a certain way to please others by changing the way you look! Instead of focusing on how each of you look, the best way to maintain a healthy relationship is to understand and embrace each others' personalities, desires, and values. The way you look might attract you to someone, but who you are will keep them around.

Date Nights

Much like family gatherings, date nights often include some element of food. You might go to the movies and be offered popcorn or a hot dog, go to a funfair and pass by a donut or ice cream truck, or you could simply be invited to a restaurant. All of these common dates would probably strike fear into your heart, making you decline a lot of the time, so you could end up spending less and less time together which will put a strain on any relationship. If you do go out together however, you might decide to always order very small amounts of food with few calories. For example, when I was on dates with my boyfriend, I would always order the Caesar salad and he would order the T-bone steak, so eating less than him was considered normal. Furthermore, ordering the salad as a girl is seen as the 'girly' thing to do, so again, my disorder was never really acknowledged or addressed.

When going on a date, most people want to make an effort with how they look. They naturally want to look beautiful and confident to visually impress their date. If you struggle with self-esteem along with your anorexia, this is a near impossible task. You'd probably spend hours deliberating over what to wear in order to look your best, but fail to find anything suitable because of your insecurities or dysmorphia, and you may even cancel the date for that reason. Unfortunately, this can make you an unreliable date and your partner may end up missing out on events or losing money, which can be frustrating.

A good way to overcome both of these challenges is to plan your dates together ahead of time instead of being spontaneous, at least while you are still recovering. This will ensure that you can plan what outfit you'll feel comfortable wearing, mentally prepare for the social setting you'll be in, and look at the online menu together before booking a table. This way, you can do your best to pick something different to eat without the pressure of time or being around other people. Your partner will then help you commit to eating this new dish by holding you accountable when you get there. This gentle encouragement and support from your partner can make all the difference and they might even join you in trying something new too!

Boys Will Be Boys

If you are dating or want to date boys, this can come with a few challenges when it comes to discussing anorexia. This is because boys tend to have their own struggles and may not appreciate certain struggles you are going through as a girl. They may also simply behave in ways that are completely normal for young boys, but because of your sensitivity, might trigger your disorder through no fault of their own. So let's explore this.

Although there is a lot of pressure for girls and women to look a certain way in society, there is also pressure for boys and men to look a certain way too. In order to be considered masculine, society usually dictates that they should be noticeably fit with a six pack and muscular arms, strong both physically and mentally, and good at sports with lots of energy. In order to achieve this, some boys may work out regularly and take a lot of pride in their appearance, so if you are dating someone like this, their need to maintain their own body could then rub off on you. You might see them working out every day which will trigger you into thinking that you need to do the same, regardless of your current body type. This can be unhealthy and even dangerous because we all have our own different physical needs, so competing in this way could lead to injury, excessive weight loss, or fatigue.

Some boys might also like the idea of you being smaller than them. Words such as 'cute,' 'petite,' or 'sweet' are often used to describe girls they are attracted to, and they all allude to being small and slim. This might make you feel the need to live up to these descriptions in order to attract and maintain a boyfriend. Some say that boys prefer this size difference so that they come across as the dominant, protective, and masculine one in the relationship, so having a girlfriend that is larger than them is seen as emasculating. This can be a huge trigger for girls suffering with anorexia because it suggests that being curvy or larger is manly and as a young teen girl who is exploring her femininity, this can be devastating. It can then lead to conscious and rapid weight loss as a way to avoid this situation.

Males are generally very bad at seeking help when they feel ill and very rarely go to the doctors, even if they are experiencing serious symptoms; nearly two-thirds of them say they avoid going to the doctor as long as possible and 37% say that if they do attend, they withhold information (Campbell, 2019). Dr. Tisha Rowe says that reasons for this include fear, superhero syndrome, and not wanting to be seen as vulnerable. This nonchalant attitude towards health could then pass on to you and they might not take your feelings, concerns, or symptoms seriously. For example, I recall feeling light-headed and short of breath with a racing heart when at school. I told my boyfriend how I felt, but he just shrugged and told me to calm down. I eventually recovered, but this was a warning sign from my body, so it should have been taken seriously, yet I felt as though he didn't really care or understand how scary it was. Sadly, even if a boy is genuinely concerned about you, because of the male role society has created, they might still find it hard to express this in fear of looking weak or emotional, so many will just not say anything, brush it off like my boyfriend did, or even rather break up with you! This is sad, not just for you as a partner, but also for them because it could lead to serious detachment and communication issues in the future.

But don't worry, most boys do have a soft spot and if they genuinely care about you, they will have a protective energy and want to see you feeling better, even if they don't know the full story of your anorexia. They will do the work and research required to be a supportive partner and embrace a more nurturing type of masculinity that will help you to thrive.

LGBTQ+ Love

If you are part of the LGBTQ+ community, dating and finding love might feel very difficult for you because you are likely to be constantly surrounded by heteronormative examples of love, which can make you feel like an outsider. Some LGBTQ+ people suffering from anorexia who live in a state in which homosexuality is not tolerated can also carry a lot of shame, guilt, or even self-hate because of their sexuality, so these feelings of not belonging can lead to starvation as a form of self-punishment.

Sadly, this means that teens from this community are at a greater risk developing of eating disorders or negative eating habits than their heterosexual and cisgender counterparts because they tend to experience greater amounts of stress due to homophobia and prejudice: Approximately 54% of LGBT adolescents have been diagnosed with an eating disorder during their lifetime (Parker & Harriger, 2020).

This shocking statistic is concerning, but you must remember that there are helplines and community guardians out there such as The Trevor Project who can not only help you tackle your eating disorder, but also any other discriminatory challenges and injustices you are facing. With their support, validation, and extremely welcoming and affirming environments, you will be able to build a strong foundation as an LGBTQ+ teen, which will then help your anorexia recovery seem more achievable.

HEALING THROUGH LOVE LANGUAGES

When in a relationship, your recovery from anorexia should be a team effort and the key to working together positively is understanding. Knowing what each other needs to thrive and feel loved alongside other treatment is so important and this is known as understanding your "love language."

In 1992, author Gary Chapman published the book *The Five Love Languages*. In it, he explores the idea that there are five main ways in which people express and want to receive love; they are words of affirmation, quality time, physical touch, acts of service, and receiving gifts. Once you discover what both yours and your partner's preferred language is, it will be easier to work together to build a healthy relationship around your eating disorder and use this positive foundation as a springboard to stop anorexia in its tracks.

Words of Affirmation

If you are someone who responds well to positive reinforcement, encouragement, and uplifting quotes, words of affirmation could be your love language. With someone who suffers with anorexia, however, these words need to be chosen wisely by your partner to avoid being counterproductive. You won't want your partner to compliment the way you look too much or tell you that starving yourself and feeling low is a good thing, so instead, they should send you affirming messages about other aspects of you. For example, they could empower you by telling you how much you mean to them or how you enrich their lives. After all, they've probably chosen to be with you for other reasons outside of your appearance and this boost in confidence will eventually help you to start spending less time thinking about the disorder and more about who you are as a person.

Quality Time

If quality time is one of your love languages, you'll find yourself wanting undivided attention from your partner. This is not to be confused with smothering or becoming enmeshed with each other, but suggests that being present and attentive in each other's lives is important to you. You could add more quality time to your relationship by putting down your cell phones when you're talking, making eye contact more, and actively listening to not only each other's problems, but your wins too. This will help you both feel heard and potentially open your mind up to sharing your disorder with your partner if you haven't done so already. This quality time can also make it easier for them to detect any unhealthy eating habits and encourage you to get the help you deserve sooner.

Physical Touch

Even as someone who is self-conscious about your body, you may still crave physical affection. This can be confusing to your partner, so the key here is to be explicit with your boundaries. You might, for example, hate being touched on your stomach, but love your hair being played with, so tell them where and when you find comfort in their touch so that they can avoid triggering any anxiety. Being close to your partner in this way is totally normal and should be a pleasurable experience for you both, so with a little bit of guidance, there is no reason why you should have to miss out on something that makes you feel more connected just because you have an eating disorder.

Acts of Service

Acts like helping you run errands or offering to carry your school bags for you at the end of a long day will definitely make your heart melt if you are someone who's love language is acts of service. You will see it as a physical embodiment of emotional support and can be really helpful in your journey to anorexia recovery. This is because it develops a certain level of trust and often shows that your partner genuinely wants to make your life just that little bit easier for you. So if you notice this trait in your partner, you might have found a pretty good one!

Receiving Gifts

Similar to acts of service, gift-giving can be considered symbolic of love and affection and if you enjoy this, you will treasure not only the item, but the time and effort your partner has put into finding and presenting it to you. You don't necessarily want or expect anything large or expensive, but it's often the thought that counts or its sentimental value. It tells you that your partner has thought about you even when you weren't around and this compassion can be a great sign that they are considerate of your feelings. Consideration is an important trait to have when in a relationship with an anorexia sufferer because, although they may not be able to directly relate to the disorder, being empathetic and helpful will make the road to recovery feel a lot less lonely.

Love is so complex, even without the complications an eating disorder can bring to it, so if you do have a partner, know that it's completely normal to not have all the answers and solutions for a long-term relationship right now. You are still young with a lifetime of lessons to learn, so as long as you are trying to make a conscious effort while addressing any negative elements that need working on or removing, a good relationship will be very beneficial to your recovery.

SCHOOL AND EXTRACURRICULAR ACTIVITIES

School provides you with a lot of the skills you will need to thrive as a working adult. Education is the key to many opportunities in life, so for the majority of the population, it is seen as a huge and important part of who they are and doing well academically is fundamental to their self-development. However, for others, being at school can be one of the most challenging times in life because of the social aspects, the pressure of exams and achieving good grades, and dealing with authority and boundaries. If you suffer from anorexia, you might have perfectionist tendencies too, so struggling with certain subjects might feel more devastating to you than it would to the average person. Building good relationships with teachers and peers may also be challenging because of your lack of trust.

Fortunately, there are plenty of optional activities that are linked to school which can positively influence and enrich your life without the academic strains. For example, when I was suffering from anorexia in school, I threw myself into cheerleading. It kept my mind occupied and gave me temporary comfort because it was something I excelled in. Being involved in extracurricular activities like this will help you build skills that cannot be learned in an academic environment thus making you a well-rounded individual. They can help strengthen your mind, body, and soul, expand your social circle in fun ways, and build good time management skills as you learn to balance them with your school work. You might just need to choose your activities carefully because when you have anorexia, they can either be a help or hindrance to your disorder management and recovery.

SPORTS

Team sports, such as volleyball, basketball, and soccer, have a high level of competitiveness and a high-pressure nature as the aim is to be able to perform at your best at all times and win competitions. This will help you to stay fit and maintain good cardiovascular health, and being part of a team can be a great way to meet like-minded people. You are therefore likely to gain a great sense of comradery and develop teamwork skills that will be useful for the rest of your life. The pressure to constantly perform well in matches, however, can be a trigger to those with eating disorders as it can make you anxious about failure. You might start to become obsessed with winning, no matter what, and overtrain to achieve this, which can lead to excessive weight loss and poor eating habits.

Furthermore, if you take part in a majority female sport, they tend to also have an underlying emphasis on how you look or have seemingly sexist or objectifying rules around what you can and cannot wear. An example of this would be how the female handball uniforms were scrutinized in 2021. In July 2021, the Norwegian women's beach handball team was fined by the European Handball Federation after choosing to wear shorts instead of bikini bottoms during a game. Despite the fact that the bikinis were deemed too revealing for some of the players, especially for those on their periods, and the fact that men were allowed to wear long shorts, the federation proceeded to fine them, even though it had no bearing on their sporting performance or safety. After much media attention and criticism from the public, the rules were eventually changed in the female player's favor, but it shows that in some sports, there are archaic rules around female bodies that could be harmful, especially if you are someone who has sensitivity to body image or eating disorders. Revealing or tightfitting uniforms can be triggers, so bear this in mind when looking at your options or make sure you speak to your coach about how you feel before, during, and after training sessions.

If you are interested in male-dominated sports such as soccer or basketball, joining a team can be a great opportunity to show that girls can be just as successful and talented as their male peers. Great players such as forward Alex Morgan, midfielder Carli Lloyd, and Seattle Storm basketball player Suzanne Bird have paved the way for aspiring young female players and inspired many teens to get involved in these sports as extracurricular activities, which could eventually lead to being drafted to play professionally. However, outsiders may question female players' femininity purely because of their involvement in the sport and, as a teenager, this can be hard to face. It can lead to feelings of insecurity or low body confidence as you become faced with stereotypes and preconceived ideas about sports players and could cause you to want to become hyperfeminine to counterbalance the perception. Some sufferers may do this by losing weight or overemphasizing their sexuality; neither of which are healthy and could lead to dangerous situations and mental trauma. So instead, do your best to ignore the critique because if you have a talent in a particular area, you should never let outsiders stunt your potential. Also, when it comes to sports, your body is your tool and it needs fuel in order to be able to carry out all of the outstanding shots you are more than capable of achieving, so try to think of eating as a way to maintain your ability to excel in what you enjoy.

If team sports aren't appealing to you, taking part in solo sports, such as gymnastics, tennis, track, or swimming as an extracurricular activity has benefits too. They encourage self-improvement, commitment, and courage to perform on your own which are great skills for you to develop into a self-sufficient young woman. They can help you become self-motivated, responsible, and mentally tough, which are all great traits to have as a teen who is trying to combat an eating disorder. However, they do come with their own challenges that you should be aware of.

Taking part in track and field in particular can have a triggering effect on those who suffer with anorexia because of its "lighter equals faster" culture (Justice & Karpen, 2021). Coaches may notice that you are losing weight, but see it as a positive thing or an indication of athletic prowess because the less extra weight you are carrying, the easier it is to be faster. This means that your eating disorder may be overlooked and, instead, be considered as competitive and beneficial weight loss. This can be detrimental to your recovery and health in general and is a mindset that the running community regularly struggles with even up to professional levels, with some athletes saying that coaches may never specifically say that you should lose weight but it is implied through their choice of words and training techniques (Justice & Karpen, 2021). Eating disorders are also prevalent among teens who take part in swimming for similar reasons.

Martial arts and contact sports such as boxing require high levels of discipline and skill. Some people with anorexia may find comfort in this because many struggle with confidence issues and these types of sports can be used as a great way to develop a sense of achievement, pride, and focus. Others, however, may hide their disorder in these sports' discipline and explain their poor eating habits or weight loss away as perfectionism and professionalism. There is also a perception of martial artists as being strong and completely fit, so anything that challenges this idea, like an eating disorder, can be hidden away in fear of being seen as weak. But talking about having an eating disorder is far from a weakness; it's a sign of mental and emotional courage, so I would encourage you to speak to your coach about how you can balance training alongside a healthy lifestyle. Afterall, you wouldn't want to risk having no energy or muscle mass to fight!

With any of these individual sports, you may also face some feelings of loneliness, and if competitions don't go in your favor, you could end up blaming yourself a bit too harshly as you have no other teammates to comfort or share the responsibility with. Being on your own a lot also gives you time to overthink and potentially overtrain which can make your body and mind feel extremely weak and become less efficient during day-to-day activities. But remember, training as a soloist doesn't mean you are completely alone; your coach and other participants are your team and will be cheering you on from the sidelines and will be there to support you if you ever feel overwhelmed.

In general, sports are positive, exciting, and healthy ways to spend your free time and if you excel in them, they can feel very rewarding. So this is not about putting you off taking part in them, but rather making you aware of the hidden triggers that surround them so that you can make an informed decision and use them as a form of healing rather than suffering.

CHEERLEADING

Cheerleading is a great way to build sisterhoods and friendships because it requires trust and teamwork in order to not only be performed impressively, but also safely. If you come from a difficult background or are living in a negative home environment, these teams can also provide a safe space and escape for you to be yourself freely. Being part of a cheer team can help you to develop good leadership skills if you reach a position of authority and learn to listen to both your teammates and coach well, which are great transferable skills. At times, teams may feel a bit like a sorority and your coach can be an inspiration for living a healthy and active lifestyle as you get older. Cheerleading also promotes physical endurance and excellence with high-energy routines, tumbles, jumps, and stunts that require strength, flexibility, coordination, and stamina at higher levels than many other athletes. A lot of cheerleaders therefore have to maintain a healthy lifestyle outside of practice in order to be able to execute these movements throughout the season, so your coaches are likely to encourage looking after your body in the best way possible.

However, despite the release of happy hormones when you are cheering, there is unfortunately a dark side to this competitive sport, as shown in programs like Netflix's documentary series *Cheer*. During the show, there was an emphasis on weight which highlighted that, in some teams, there is pressure for athletes to be lean, toned, strong, yet also light if they are to be at the top of pyramids, for example. This can trigger unhealthy obsessions as you strive to be chosen for shows or certain stunts. Coach Monica Aldama made it clear that although performance and skill are the most important aspects of cheerleading, curating a 'look' was also important and her standards were high. There was a perception that team members needed to be a certain size in order to look good in uniforms, so much so that in one episode female cheerleaders expressed their nerves about the team weigh-in. Some even mentioned feeling the need to restrict their food intake to reach or maintain the required weight to be able to perform. There was also a need to have each of the girl's hair a certain way for competitions, so if they didn't have long or straight enough hair, it could make them feel as though their body image is lacking in some way. With this in mind, it is unsurprising that as many as 45% of female athletes exhibit some kind of disordered eating behaviors (Schurrer, 2020).

The constant cardio training received through cheerleading will mean that participants will naturally lose weight, but when coupled with little time to have nutritious meals between practices and studying, it can often cross the line from natural weight loss to unhealthy malnutrition. Team members will usually grab something small or nothing at all as they try to fit eating around their busy schedules, which could risk losing muscle as well as fat and this is detrimental to normal bodily functioning.

There is also an inference that cheerleaders should also be popular at school. This idea is reinforced in movies like *Senior Year*, where teenager Stephanie makes it her mission to be well-known and at the top of the school girl hierarchy by becoming a great dancer and captain of the cheerleading team. The pressure to be popular and fit the image of a typical cheerleader can turn you into a bit of a people pleaser, which can make you feel inauthentic and detached from your true self and, as we know, this lack of self can result in a loss of appetite and depression.

CREATIVITY

If you are a naturally creative person, developing this skill through extracurricular activities can seem like a natural next step. Creative expression can improve your mood as it induces the production of dopamine in the brain which is a natural antidepressant. Whether it be writing a story, doodling little characters, or singing your favorite song, all of these things can help you feel good from the inside out. In fact, studies show that taking part in a creative activity just once a day can lead to a more positive outlook on life and instant gratification (Brightwater Group, 2019). It can also boost your self-esteem because you are essentially showing that you can make something out of 'nothing.' Being creative also improves cognitive function and can alleviate stress and anxiety because when absorbed in an activity, you tend to forget your worries and negative thoughts, so why not get involved in something creative to nourish your mental health and, in turn, your eating disorder?

For example, you could join a music class. This can be particularly beneficial to your mental and emotional health, especially if you are a naturally shy person because you can let the instrument do the 'talking' for you. Music can enable you to express yourself in ways you might usually find difficult in everyday life. For instance, the flute could express the fluid and soothing tones you feel when you are calm, whereas the drums may be a way to release the chaos going on in your mind, loudly and confidently. A lot of musicians like Adele or Taylor Swift use music cathartically in this way and always seem to wear their hearts on their sleeves when it comes to songwriting. For Adele, she has said that she uses music to share her experiences, release her worries and concerns, and lighten the load in her mind, so you could do the same through writing your own songs. You also never know where a hidden talent like this could lead you!

According to Frontiers in Psychiatry and their 2021 study into music and anorexia, those suffering from this disorder described making or listening to music as a welcome distraction and a way to combat loneliness. They would also consider attending music therapy as a form of treatment. One patient in this study said that being involved in a band or music class gave them something to commit to when struggling with motivation and used it as a form of bonding with other patients when they performed together (Priya et al., 2021). They said that listening or creating a sad piece of music, however, could become a trigger and would cause them to mirror the emotions heard in the music, so choosing what music you listen to or make wisely is also important.

As a sufferer, you will probably be tired of having to conform to certain spoken or unspoken rules about how you should and shouldn't look or what you can and cannot eat, so art classes or creating art on your own time can be used as an escape from these restrictions and feel quite freeing because there is no right or wrong way to create it. Art is considered the purest form of self-expression as it doesn't need to be 'perfect' and furthermore, it doesn't even need to be understood by anyone else but you, making it a potentially low-pressure pastime. Because of this freedom of expression and the benefits many feel after engaging in it, art has even been used in clinical settings since the 1940s as a form of therapy and has since been recognized for its healing benefits for treating eating disorders in particular. It was found that engaging in creative processes like painting, photography, or drawing utilizes, trains, and improves the way the heart, nerves, and brain work, so it can amazingly reverse the damage caused by disorders such as anorexia (Misluk, n.d.). Some mental health providers, such as counselors, social workers, and psychologists, use art to gain a better understanding of their clients because one's art is said to reveal subconscious thoughts and can therefore act as a bridge to conversation.

A great example of how art can ease some of the mental struggles of anorexia is the work of Norwegian photographer Lene Marie Fossen who used photography during her battle with the disorder. She was completely open about her body and disorder and often made herself the subject of the images she produced. Not only did her art open up the conversation around body image, eating disorders, and the human experience in general, but she also described it as an asset to her own healing process. Fossen told audiences in a 2017 interview that she'd developed anorexia as a 10 year old when she became fearful of growing up; she tried to stop time by not eating with the hope that she wouldn't go through puberty (TEDx Talks, 2017). After years of treatment, she learned that attempting to stop time and her aging process in this way was very dangerous and unhealthy, so she decided to try to achieve it another way–through photography. She saw taking photos as a way of capturing moments in time that would never happen again and saw real beauty in this sense of timelessness. Although she was unable to fully recover and sadly passed away in 2019, she said that she was proud to be able to express herself in this way and that it provided a much needed release for the mental struggles and physical pains that came with her eating disorder.

The performing arts are another form of creative expression that you may come across as an after school activity. Singing, dancing, and acting require a certain level of confidence but enable you to become a different person or character for a few hours and leave your anorexia behind during this time. School drama clubs in particular are often places where one's talent is more important than body image too, as characters in musicals, for example, come in all shapes and sizes, so there should be parts for everyone to feel comfortable playing, which can make you feel accepted. However, the audition process isn't for the fainthearted. If you audition for a particular part and aren't successful, it can lead to self-doubt which is a potential trigger for eating disorders, so you do need to have tough skin in order to keep trying and the mental resilience to continue working on your craft and strive for the roles you desire. Just because you didn't get the role this time doesn't mean you can't try again next year, and the fact that you were unsuccessful isn't a reflection of you as a person, but simply circumstance. Your talent will shine through, regardless of the role you get!

ACADEMIC CLUBS OR COURSES

If you have a very academic mind, you might enjoy clubs such as math, debate, or book clubs, despite them being very similar to your regular lessons during school hours. Advanced or honors courses can provide a more in-depth understanding of certain topics, support your learning in subjects that you may struggle with in normal class settings, or maybe even help you to become an expert in your chosen field.

Attending a mathematics club may not be for everyone, but if you do enjoy it, it will not only teach you about algebra and triangles, but it will aid the development of more general motor and problem-solving skills. Debate club will help you develop your oral and written communication, critical thinking skills, learn effective ways to research, be organized, and present to a group. These are all great qualities to have which will give you a more rounded view of the world and could even make you feel confident enough to explore your eating disorder in an academic way. Exploring anorexia in this way will allow you to think more critically about your behavior and learn that you are not alone, which will hopefully lead you to a resolution along with the support of your like-minded and open-minded peers and tutors. You'll also learn how to express how you feel articulately which will give you more of a chance of getting the support you need.

Because these types of extracurricular activities are quite similar to school work, however, they do come with their own triggers. They may start to become seen as an extension of the school day and apply too much pressure on top of existing tests, projects, and college applications. Within the school curriculum, teens are already encouraged to think ahead and academically prepare themselves for life's milestones which contributes to stress, so to add to more pressure on top of this can have a negative effect on your mental health. This increased pressure can lead to obsession with grades, anxiety, extreme competitiveness, changes in appetite, sleep difficulties, social isolation and more, which all have direct links to eating disorders, so be mindful about adding to your workload in this way. The time you spend researching for debates or completing extra homework could also distract you from eating enough food and you might start to focus on your performance rather than the interior problem. So to avoid this, you should have a clear schedule that allows time for healthy practices and rest too.

COMMUNITY PROJECTS

Community service helps teens like you acquire compassion and life skills while providing a service to people who need it most. It will give you the opportunity to become active members of society and develop a special bond with the community around you while improving the way the neighborhood looks and feels for all. On the surface, this is a selfless act, but getting out into the community can also help you to put your disorder and weight into perspective. You'll see more lifestyles, body types, and weights than you'll ever see at school and probably come to realize that you are not abnormal or weird in any way, but rather just struggling with something beyond your control, as many others are. As well as this, being involved in community projects reduces the risk of social isolation, especially if you already feel distant from your classmates. You'll be meeting new people every week and practicing your social skills every time, so you will have more chances to meet new friends who you can build fresh connections with, without the pressure of seeing them everyday at school. This can also open the doors to new experiences, conversations, and ideas. You might even come across other teens who are also suffering with anorexia and use this as an opportunity to listen to their stories as a way of healing and gaining different perspectives on the condition. If you're brave enough, you could even speak about your own battles without the fear of it being passed around school.

However, I know that entering unknown territory and meeting new people isn't an easy step for many suffering with anorexia and I wouldn't want you to end up focusing on other people and forget about your own needs, so take your time and try to find projects that work for you. You could take literal baby steps and work with babies or very young children who won't judge or ask questions, or even work with animals who have been proven to reduce stress just by looking at or stroking them!

Research on human-animal interactions is still relatively new, but some studies have shown positive health effects that are beneficial to anorexia recovery. It decreases levels of cortisol in the body which is a stress-related hormone, and these interactions also lower blood pressure, so volunteering at a pet shop or farm could be a great place to start. Coaching or looking after younger kids turns you into a role model and this responsibility can make you not want to let them down by slipping into unhealthy habits, so it could become the inspiration you need to get you on the road to recovery. Garden or farming projects can help you to learn the origins of different produce without it being too overwhelmingly related to eating and can make food seem less scary or negative if this is something you are finding difficult to overcome.

This shows that there are many projects out there that can suit your needs and even be a positive influence on your anorexia recovery journey. Whatever you decide to do in the community, when you leave school, or even before then, you are bound to reap the benefits, so my advice is to dive in and explore with the knowledge that you are going to be in safe hands.

GOVERNMENT, LEADERSHIP, AND MEDIA

Being part of your school government can really help you make a difference in your school community. You'll be able to collaboratively work out ways in which you can keep students safe and happy in a learning environment while gaining knowledge of the greater workings of the United States government as a whole, which could potentially leave you feeling empowered enough to make changes in your own wider community. You could even use this extracurricular activity to find out what policies are in place and what support is available to students with anorexia at your school, which will either reassure you that you are not alone in your battle or highlight that more needs to be done to help. Fortunately, you'll be in a position to make these changes and make not only your own school life more manageable, but also the lives of your peers and future students. By taking on this responsibility, you'll develop leadership skills, eventually grow in confidence, and learn that your voice has power which are useful assets to have when managing anorexia symptoms and going through treatment.

Joining your school's media team can be beneficial if you have dreams of becoming a journalist, or simply if you enjoy writing and sharing information. You'll be able to write articles in the school newspaper, be one of the school's radio or television presenters, or work on creating a movie and as part of the production, you will need to carry out research via wider sources of media. This research will open your eyes to national and global issues and can help to make you less naive and more critical about what you see on mainstream news outlets and on social media. You'll learn that the media can be a tool for change, but also that as consumers, we need to be wary about what we see, absorb, and believe because, of course, not all news is good news. Tasks like these can be helpful to people suffering from anorexia because they can develop critical thinking skills and instill the ability to filter out false, harmful, or triggering content from one's own media exposure. It will also make what you do see less influential on you and reduce the chance of it leading you towards unhealthy behavior. For example, if you see an advertisement for weight loss pills on television, you will be more likely to be able to critically assess the advert, recognize its intent and potential downfalls, and avoid being emotionally drawn to or triggered by it.

However, if you aren't used to this level of exposure to the media, this heightened awareness can come with a risk of panic and anxiety. You might come across content that you wouldn't necessarily have done before more frequently and start to think negatively about the current state of affairs. You may start to realize that the world is such a big place and, as a teenager, this can feel overwhelming and make you feel like you have little control over what's happening around you. As we know, feeling out of control in this way can then lead to you wanting to micromanage your food intake in an unhealthy way. So if you do find yourself feeling overwhelmed by your research, try to make sure that you have a healthy balance of awareness and distance. Limit your media exposure by reading or watching the news for only 30 minutes per day or work as a team so that information is relayed rather than sourced firsthand, until you feel ready to investigate on your own. Media and politics need more females involved to provide balanced perspectives, so you shouldn't let your eating disorder discourage you from this opportunity.

RELIGIOUS GROUPS

If you belong to a religion, joining a group that studies and practices its teachings can be a comfort. Many people use religion as a positive way to deal with stress, provide a basis of self-worth and values, and draw strength from because its spiritual texts can often be a source of inspiration and guidance. Being part of a religion can also bring about a strong sense of community which can help if you feel isolated at times. As well as this, many faiths view the body as a sacred and divine creation by a higher power, so they believe it should be treated with care and respect. Therefore, if you are someone who suffers from anorexia, this concept can be a huge incentive to recover.

On the other hand, if your religion is quite strict, it can make you worry about disappointing the community, yourself, and your God if you feel as though you are unable to live up to the values of the faith. This can bring about feelings of guilt, depression, and even fear which are significant triggers for anorexia. Many religions also engage in fasting and restrictive dieting as part of their practices. For example, Muslims practice fasting during the holy month of Ramadan, Christians during Lent, and Jewish people during Yom Kippur, all with the goal of becoming closer to God, becoming spiritually mature, or to demonstrate discipline and control. This can make it hard to engage in religious practices healthily if you are already struggling to eat regularly and are vulnerable to eating disorders. Similarly, there are also times in religious calendars, such as Christmas and Eid, that encourage and celebrate eating and food, so this can be particularly difficult to bear. Fortunately, most religious groups will be completely understanding if there are any medical reasons why you aren't able to partake in such practices or ceremonies, so the best thing to do is to be honest and open about your condition and get the support you need. They will be able to suggest other ways of making a sacrifice because after all, your religious leaders will want to help fuel your recovery, not make the struggle more difficult.

PART-TIME JOBS

Starting paid employment is a natural progression into your teen and young adult years. It is a great way to exercise independence and responsibility while learning about money management and taking control of your life in ways that many suffering from anorexia crave. A part-time job does, however, take up a lot of time when juggling it with school, so be careful not to take on too many hours so that you have enough time to rest, refresh your mind, and, most importantly, eat. Designate some time in your week for self-care to ensure that you are able to do all the things that keep you healthy and work backwards from there to see how much time you can actually afford to put into work before you sign the contract. For example, if you are at school for six hours per day, have hockey and drama club twice a week for four hours per week, and need eight hours of sleep each night along with time for travel, homework, and social events with friends and family, you probably wouldn't want to take on a contract that was anything more than eight hours per week. This will prevent you from feeling overwhelmed with pressure or skipping meals in order to accommodate your busy schedule. Your health should be your main priority, and after all, you will have your entire life to work and make the money you want.

Employers also need a level of reliability, so getting a grip on your disorder and mental health is important before you apply so that you can be a dependable employee. Although your manager may be empathetic to what you're going through, in order to run a successful business, they will need staff who can perform well regularly, so days off for feeling unwell may not be tolerated if it happens too often. So, try to be realistic with what you can give and do your best to stay motivated and commit to those few hours of work, otherwise you might find it difficult to maintain employment. The buzz of getting your first paycheck will be worth it!

SPARE TIME

If you decide not to enroll in any extracurricular activities or part-time employment, you might end up with a lot of free time on your hands. This can be used as some much deserved 'you' time and relaxation, but too much time spent doing nothing could work against you. The COVID-19 pandemic lockdowns are interesting examples of this, with research from this period showing that boredom, stress, and a lack of social interaction or community services led to unhealthy eating habits and even a surge in children and young people reporting eating disorders; The Royal College of Psychiatrists in Scotland found that treatment referrals for eating disorders tripled between 2018 and 2021 (BBC News, 2021). Harvard Health Publishing also found that approximately 35% of people lost a significant amount of weight during this time and put it down to stress making them miss hunger cues, but few people complain about weight loss, so this number could be higher than reported.

Sadly, a mother in Scotland experienced this firsthand when the lockdowns had a huge negative impact on her daughter's anorexia. She found that without being at school and feeling isolated from her peers at home, the illness thrived and within a few weeks she deteriorated quickly (BBC News, 2021). This is because eating disorders often thrive off loneliness, so keeping yourself occupied and around your peers with extracurricular activities, at least some of the time, will be helpful.

For others, the lockdown led to weight gain; patient data showed that 39% of people gained more than the natural fluctuation of two and a half pounds (Pegg Frates, 2021). This was also largely due to stress (because people respond to stress in different ways) and the "buffet blitz" phenomenon, where we started constantly consuming a higher amount of fatty and salty foods because of boredom and the lack of access to healthy produce. No access to gyms also meant that people's metabolism slowed down and it was far easier to put on weight that you normally wouldn't gain, even if you maintained a healthy diet. This probably meant that you were or still are slightly curvier than you were a few years ago or are surrounded by people who have put on weight and this could trigger anxiety. You might start to worry that you look fat and are losing control of your body, so you might try to counterbalance this with undereating and filling your time with exercise. If you don't have much else to do, you may also start to compare your daily routine and appearance to others and become lost in comparison culture, which, as we know, is sadly a common trigger for anorexia.

Ultimately, spare time is no bad thing and is necessary for a balanced and fulfilling life, but if you do decide to fill it, you should make sure you do it wisely and manageably to avoid slipping into any unhealthy patterns.

6

TREATMENT

Whether you have been suffering from anorexia for days, months, or years, the negativity it brings to your life doesn't have to last forever. As someone who has suffered from it and came out the other side, I want you to know that there is help available to you and by getting the right support as soon as possible, you will be able to recover well and live a healthy life into adulthood–it's never too late. Acknowledging that you have a problem has been the first step, so now it's time to reach out and move forward with a clean slate and open arms to embrace a new way of living and thinking.

ASKING FOR HELP

Seeking help is probably the hardest step to make once you realize you have an eating disorder. It is not only an acknowledgment that something isn't right, but it's also an acceptance that you are unable to find relief on your own at the moment. It takes so much courage to get through this stage, but once there, you will feel like a load has been lifted and start to see the light at the end of the tunnel.

There is no right or wrong time to reach out for support, but it's usually best to choose a quieter time so you won't get distracted or rushed and a private place so that you don't feel anxious about anyone else overhearing what you have to say. How you start the conversation is completely up to you, but it's a good idea to first let the person know that what you are about to tell them is important to you and a sensitive topic. That way, they can also prepare themselves to take you seriously. Don't worry, your words might not make sense straight away, and if they don't, the person you have confided in will most likely ask questions to help you come to a mutual understanding. As long as you stay true to yourself and do your best to express yourself, that's enough and you can always clarify anything else later. You might cry, stammer, lose your words, or get frustrated, but all of this is completely normal. Just be patient with yourself and keep going. You'll also need to be patient with the person you are telling because they might not know how to respond to you straight away as it will be a lot to absorb and they might not know much about the disorder. To prepare for this, you could bring some leaflets with you or have a website about anorexia ready on your phone as this could act like a springboard to bounce off of if you feel stuck when describing what it is you are suffering with.

A simple suggested guide to follow when asking for help is:

1. Explain how you feel in as much depth as possible.
2. Tell the person you choose to talk to why this is concerning you and how it affects your daily life.
3. Be specific with how you want them to help. Do you want them to accompany you to a hospital or doctor appointment? Do you want them to assist you with self-help techniques? Or do you simply want them to listen and take no action just yet?

PROFESSIONAL SUPPORT

Once you've reached out for help, the next step will be to learn how to improve symptoms and get treated. Managing an eating disorder is no easy task. It usually takes long-term commitment and you will probably need to visit centers and your treatment team regularly, even if your disorder and other related health problems seem under control on the surface. There are several layers to anorexia with your eating habits being just the tip of the iceberg, so healing will take patience, energy, and hard work, but it is all worth it.

Your treatment team will be made up of a few different professionals who specialize in eating disorders and your nearest and dearest. The team members are likely to include a mental health professional such as a psychologist and/or psychiatrist who will provide mental therapy and/or medication prescriptions, a dietitian who will help you with meal planning and educate you on the best foods for nutrition and recovery, a medical or dental specialist who will treat any related problems that have arisen due to your anorexia, and a parent or guardian for additional emotional support and guidance. It is important that everyone involved communicates well so that if you require any adjustments to your treatment, everybody can offer the right amount and type of support to keep you on track for recovery.

Once you have your team together, a plan will be made to cater to your specific needs. Goals will be set, with your input, and you'll be supported at every step of the way to help you stick with it. Your team can also help you to find resources available in your area and identify affordable treatment options that match your family's financial situation.

Therapy

Psychological therapy is the most important part of anorexia treatment because anorexia is a condition that stems from the way we think. Regular sessions can go on for months or years, with the aim of helping you normalize your eating and thinking patterns in order to achieve a healthier weight and state of mind. You'll learn to build new positive habits into your routine, let out any concerns and fears, and explore healthier ways to cope with stressful life situations. It is impossible to completely avoid stress in life, so therapy will just help you find ways to make it easier for you to cope with it when it arises, without restricting your food intake, feeling depressed, and becoming overly anxious.

One type of therapy you are likely to be introduced to is cognitive behavioral therapy (CBT) which focuses on addressing the way you act, think, and feel towards challenging situations in life. When used to treat eating disorders specifically, it is sometimes called enhanced cognitive behavior therapy (CBT-E) because it will be highly detailed and individualized to your particular eating disorder and life circumstances. It will help you to recognize the unhealthy patterns you are building and the triggers that ignite them and bring you back to a truer sense of reality, which can help you combat body dysmorphia. CBT-E is usually carried out on a one-to-one basis, twice a week, and starts with you and your therapist gaining a mutual understanding of your problems and concerns about weight. They'll then make sure that you understand the impact anorexia has had on your body, mental state, and loved ones, and teach you about different body images and moods while recognizing any triggers you may have faced before you sought help. Finally, you will be encouraged to envisage ways you can make yourself healthy and happy again, with their support. Your first few sessions won't be easy, but stick with it; your therapist is there to help you and will find ways to make the rest of the sessions as comfortable and productive as possible.

Another type of therapy you could be offered is family-based therapy (FBT), which takes place with your immediate family or guardians with the aim of helping them learn and develop ways in which they can support you in the home until you are able to do it on your own. It is sometimes referred to as Maudsley Family Therapy because it was a technique initially developed at the Maudsley Hospital in London. FBT is usually more cost-effective than other forms of therapy because most of the work will be done away from the hospital and by members of your family, with just a few sessions for guidance from a professional. FBT will usually start with a meal in the therapist's office, so that they can see how you interact with members of your family and the food presented to you. Once observed, you will then sit together and acknowledge any good behavior but also address any unhelpful or damaging dynamics that need to be changed. Finally, your family will be given tips on how to plan, prepare, serve, and supervise the eating of nourishing and energy-rich meals at home. Being treated at home in this way means that you don't have to compete with any other patients in hospital or treatment centers and, because of this undivided attention, you might find that you start to notice a difference in your weight and mental state quite quickly. FBT is recognized as the most effective treatment for anorexia, with more that 60% of fully recovered patients crediting it as their most helpful type of therapy (Leigh, 2019).

Group therapy is another similar option but it would involve meeting with professionals and other people who have eating disorders rather than your family. This can be useful for gaining other perspectives from people who can relate to your intricate struggles personally. It can relieve feelings of isolation and feel like a safe space to talk without fear of judgment. Group therapy does, however, come with some risks, as being around others with the same disorder as you can trigger you or make your eating habits seem normal, so your progress is likely to be monitored by your treatment team regularly.

On top of any of these therapies, you will probably be asked to do some homework, such as keeping a food journal and identifying any external influences that may be hindering your treatment progress or worsening the unhealthy eating patterns you are trying to rectify. On review, your therapist will then be able to work out ways to eliminate these things from your life, at least temporarily, until you are well enough to combat them head on.

Supervised Weight Gain

Weight gain is an essential part of the recovery process if you have lost a lot and it all starts with education. Your nutritionist will teach you the value of different foods and why they are important to your natural growth and functioning, with the aim of persuading you to eat healthily and slowly increase your calorie intake in order to put on enough body fat and muscle to be considered healthy for your age and height. You'll also learn the different ways your current eating habits are negatively affecting your body and sometimes, these cold hard facts can be just the intervention you need to shock you into changing your lifestyle. You'll be taught how to plan meals, usually three main meals a day with regular snacks in between, and take brave steps to avoid dieting.

It may take quite a long time for this new way of eating and thinking about food to become second nature, especially if you've been suffering from anorexia for a long time, and your body will need time to readjust because it has become accustomed to nutritional deprivation and low food intake. Your stomach may also have shrunk which will make you feel full

TREATMENT

quicker, so you might be unable to maintain your prescribed meal plan straight away. If this happens, don't worry, your nutritionist will adjust it but be aware that you will need to push through some difficulties like this in order to get better.

Once you manage to eat more, you might experience some physical side effects, such as bloating, constipation, and headaches. You could also experience some mental and emotional side effects such as anxiety as you get used to seeing your body change. These feelings are completely normal and often temporary, but indicate why you should always be supervised throughout this stage. Fortunately, as your body adapts to the meal plan, it will get easier for you to consume more and you will even start to feel more energized and positive about what you are doing.

So how does it work? Well, at the beginning of the weight gain program, your treatment team may start you off with the recommended calories per day for someone your age (approx 2,200–2,400 calories) because it is likely that you were eating far less than this. Once they deem you as low risk for any refeeding complications, it is not uncommon for sufferers to eventually be given a daily target of up to 5,000 calories with the aim of gaining half a pound to two pounds per week until they achieve their goal weight, especially as a teen who is still growing (Grubiak, 2022). It is so high because you are likely to have become hypermetabolic, which means that your metabolism is extremely high due to the body having been trying to rebuild all the tissue lost during starvation, so it will take a lot of calories to counterbalance this. Your body might also convert some of these calories into heat rather than tissue, making weight restoration even harder. Calories are not the only element to focus on when it comes to gaining weight, so your team will also consider nutritional value of the foods included in your plan. For example, it would be unhealthy to eat

5,000 calories worth of chocolate, so you will be provided with a plan that includes a more nutritionally balanced diet with a healthy amount of carbohydrates, protein, and 'good' fats based on your particular needs.

On average, it takes approximately 12 months to restore a healthy weight in anorexia sufferers (Grubiak, 2022) but longer to end disordered thoughts, so just because your weight is considered normal, it's imperative that you continue with your other types of treatment; recovery is about state, not just weight.

Medicine and Medical Support

There aren't any medications that cure eating disorders and the FDA has not approved any specifically for the treatment of anorexia. However, if therapy doesn't seem to be effective because of low mood or anxiety, some adults are prescribed antidepressants or anti-anxiety drugs to help them reach a place where they are more open to speaking with a therapist or to assist with weight gain and calm obsessive thinking (Smith et al., 2020). For children and teens, there is far more hesitation when it comes to using drugs in this way, so you should never self prescribe or take any medication without the consent of an adult, parent, or doctor.

Residential Treatment

If your family is unable to give you the care you require at home or you are at a high risk of relapse but not in severe medical danger, it might be best for you to stay in a rehabilitation and treatment center. Being an inpatient or receiving private treatment in this way can be very expensive as many insurance plans do not cover all costs, but you shouldn't avoid treatment because of this; your family should always talk to your treatment team about any financial concerns.

In a rehabilitation center, you would be looked after more closely than at home and be treated among other sufferers. You'd be provided with 24-hour care, structure, and access to a range of different treatments including traditional therapies and education as well as body image workshops, yoga, cooking, art, drama, and exercise when appropriate. Being away from home for long periods of time might sound daunting and you may have mixed feelings about being there, but your family will usually be able to visit you on the weekends and during holidays and carers will ensure that it is a pleasant, nurturing, and safe environment for you. Everyone there wants you to recover and, in the nicest way possible, doesn't want you to be there!

When you are first admitted, you will go through an assessment phase during which the treatment team will work out what level of care you need as it is likely that all patients will have bespoke plans, triggers, and requirements. You'd then be assigned a level and your plan will begin as soon as it is ready. In most inpatient facilities, there are also general food and daily living rules and expectations that every patient will be expected to follow as a way of ensuring that you have enough nutrients and calories to keep you on track for weight gain and equip you with the skills needed after discharge. Some of these expectations include:

- Completing all meals and snacks and abstaining from treatment interference behavior. Interference behavior is anything that is deemed to be counterproductive to your weight gain journey or mental health recovery. For example, frequent exercising, leg shaking, or purging. Leg shaking may not seem like a huge problem, but some sufferers will use this to burn extra calories.
- Attending all group sessions and participating well. In order to make the most of your stay, you will be

expected to take full advantage of the support and care available to you. That way you will be more likely to be discharged and be able to carry on with your life outside of the facility.
- Some facilities allow cell phones, but not outside of your room. This is to limit your exposure to negative influences such as social media and advertisements which could be detrimental to your recovery.
- No bullying. If you are someone who has suffered from bullying due to your disorder, this rule will be a very much welcomed one. There is usually zero tolerance to bullying because there is a firm understanding of how damaging it can be for someone who has such a serious mental health condition. You should feel safe, accepted, and comfortable with those you live with, so bullying has no place in a treatment center at all.

There may also be some other guidelines such as no fashion, exercise, or food related magazines or clothing, no revealing clothing, and no pajamas to be worn outside of sleeping hours. These are all in place to maintain a trigger free environment and get you to a place where you feel mentally strong enough to not be affected by them anymore. Just before discharge, you might then be asked to join a community reintegration program to ensure you are ready to return to a less structured living space.

Hospitalization

Being admitted to hospital on a full-time basis is usually the last resort for very severe cases of anorexia. It is only required if your body becomes so weak that you cannot carry out daily tasks, if you are physically unable to consume anything due to anorexia related ailments, or if you suffer complications from the treatment itself. The Academy of Eating Disorders also recommends that sufferers should be admitted to hospital if they are 75% below their ideal body weight as a guide but each case is treated individually. This would be considered a medical emergency and you will be kept in until you become stable (Floyd, 2020).

The most serious complication related to anorexia treatment is refeeding syndrome. Refeeding syndrome is sadly life-threatening and occurs when a considerably malnourished person begins to receive nutrition again and their body cannot restart the metabolic process (Cleveland Clinic, n.d.). They might experience swelling, heart and/or lung failure, gastrointestinal problems, weakness, and delirium. You'd be most at risk of developing this syndrome if you have less than a 70% median BMI, had little to no calorie intake for more than 10 days, have a history of refeeding syndrome, or have lost a lot of weight in a short period of time (Cleveland Clinic, n.d.). It is a very complex illness, but it's fortunately also very rare.

SELF-HELP

Remember, the most important member of your treatment team is you. Investment in your own treatment is paramount, so you need to be 100% committed and actively involved for it to work. It's best not to stray from your team's prescription for you, but it is definitely necessary to take ownership over your journey and do things to help yourself as well.

If you are an outpatient, you could find new activities to take part in that will break up your usual routine and remove yourself from past triggers. For example, you could go to the movies by yourself, find a new circle of friends outside of school, or start an online anonymous blog about your recovery. You could also start talking to more people you trust outside of your treatment team as your therapy sessions may give you the confidence to tell your friends or extended family what you are struggling with more honestly.

You should also start to change the way you speak to and about yourself. Positive self-talk plays a pivotal role in recovery and our relationship with ourselves in general. As we know, our minds are so powerful, so if you tell yourself you are weak, unpopular, and ugly, you will believe it and it will become your reality. So instead, tell yourself regularly that you have the power to overcome this illness, you have a great support network around you, and that you are confident; you will see how much this changes your attitude. Remind yourself daily that you have so much more to live for and that these tough few weeks, months, or years of treatment are just a small part of your life that will set a solid foundation for happiness.

Self-help can also come in the form of listening to your body more intently and understanding its natural distress signals as cues to take action. For example, when you have allergies, your eyes may water and you'll start to sneeze. This is your body's way of telling you that something is irritating it and you would then either take medication to stop this reaction or distance yourself from the irritant. Well, this should work in the same way for hunger or starvation; now that you are trying to recover from anorexia, instead of ignoring your body's cries in the form of hunger pains and lightheadedness like you used to, it's time to acknowledge them as signs that your body is struggling and needs fuel in order to keep functioning. You should then soothe your body by eating something nutritious and keep this natural "cue and action" going.

If you are worried about how your body is changing as you go through treatment, it is recommended by therapists that you ask your parents to hide or cover any full length mirrors around the house until you are ready to look at yourself. This will stop you from becoming too focused on your appearance which may deter you from making progress. Once you are out of what is considered a "danger weight," you could then start looking at your new body shape and will hopefully be in a position to appreciate the changes rather than fear them.

Being more careful online can be another very helpful way to support your treatment plan. Unfortunately, there is a lot of false information out there and a huge amount of triggers on social media, so it would be a good idea to delete your accounts or switch off your data or wifi for the majority of the day. Instead, when you feel bored or lonely, you could try practicing meditation and relaxation. Meditation is a great way to calm an anxious mind and reduce stress hormones in the body and some parents say that it is one of the best ways to help their child recover, as they value more holistic approaches to treatment which focus on emotional well-being, cognitive flexibility, and establishment of a meaningful life (Leigh, 2019).

RECOVERY

Everybody's anorexia treatment journey is different and it is by no means straightforward, but it's important to remember that recovery is possible. It can be smooth sailing with little to no complications or relapses, or you may regularly struggle to get your body back to a healthy state, feel very scared and anxious about your physical changes, or even slip back into old habits, but with determination and support, you can get there. Just remind yourself why you chose recovery and look forward to feeling free and truly content again.

According to Dr. Lauren Muhlheim of Eating Disorder Therapy LA, physical recovery is usually defined as when you have normalized heart rate, blood pressure, and body temperature, and when your period returns to normal if it had initially been affected. The return of your menstrual cycle is so important because it has been found to be a better indication of cognitive recovery than weight. Psychological recovery is suggested by improved mood, decreased disordered thoughts around food and weight, acknowledging normal hunger cues, and regular eating. You will also have improved social functioning and a return of interest in age appropriate activities. Full brain recovery is said to take between six months and two years, with parents describing it as seeing their child "coming out of a fog" and returning to their pre-illness selves (Muhlheim, 2020). Parents are also saying that their child should only be considered recovered if they have a positive outlook on life and feel that they want and deserve to be healthy, not just because they hit certain medical targets and figures. Furthermore, some sufferers believe that full recovery is impossible and that they will always have anorexia, but just learn how to battle and suppress its symptoms. Although, in relation to medical standards, for every four anorexia sufferers, three will make a partial recovery but just 21% are considered fully recovered (Leigh, 2019); symptom-free for at least two years. This suggested that there needs to be more work done to ensure sufferers get the treatment they need and deserve. The good news, however, is that the prognosis is better in young people who had a short illness duration; in this demographic the full recovery rate is up to 60% (National Institute of Health and Care Excellence, 2019).

What if You Relapse?

Relapsing is quite common. It is when you resort back to anorexic habits, thoughts, or self-talk and you can potentially start to lose weight again. If this does happen to you, don't panic and instead learn from it and be kind to yourself, because as long as you get back on track, it is not considered a failure. In fact, there is "recovery in relapse" as sufferer Nicole Davenport says, because during a relapse you can use it as an opportunity to learn, grow stronger, and show anorexia just how resilient you can be (Davenport, n.d.).

Because relapses are considered steps in the wrong direction, recognizing and managing them is an important part of recovery, so you should have a plan in place just in case they occur. One part of the plan could be to have a team member or professional's number at hand at all times. This could be a therapist, teacher, counselor, parent, or charity helpline because the sooner you act on during a relapse, the easier it will be to get yourself out of it. You could also make sure that you have a list of reasons why you want to recover on hand to review if and when things get difficult because it will act as a reminder to stop any damaging or counterproductive behavior. Sometimes in the early stages of recovery, it's hard to think of reasons to recover for yourself, so you could include reasons for your friends or even your pet i.e. your dog wouldn't be able to look after themselves if you weren't here and would miss your play times and cuddles, so you could do it for them initially.

If you are already in the grips of a relapse, it's essential to hold yourself accountable. Just because you may have slipped up a little (or a lot), it doesn't mean that you should throw away the weeks or months of hard work you've already put in and give up on the journey completely; stick to your commitment to get better because a one or two day pause is better than a complete stop. In this case, it might be useful to write a diary of realistic meals you are going to eat for the week and tick them off when you do them, so that the diary and your family can hold you responsible too! Music could be a therapeutic way to return to your path to recovery; something empowering and upbeat if you need motivation or something calming and slow if you need to put a halt on racing thoughts. You might also want to develop a "safe space" at home. For example, if you have a spare room or even a cubbyhole in which you go to refocus your mind. Fill it with all your favorite things; cushions, sweets, scents, and photos and go there for a shot of comfort.

Don't forget: *Healing comes in waves and maybe today the wave hits the rocks, but that's okay, darling. You are still healing.* –Ljeoma Umebinyuo

7

BLANK SLATE

So, you've made it out the other side and no longer need regular treatment or supervision for anorexia. Congratulations, but now what? How do you maintain this success and live with a body that looks and feels very different to how it did before? How do you relate to old friends and potentially make new ones with your fresh state of mind? Well, first of all, you will need to come to a place of acceptance of your new appearance and identity and start a new journey of self-love on a blank slate. At first, you might not love the idea of having more curves or being a larger clothing size than you were before, but it's something you will have to learn to live with in order to have a mentally peaceful life. The best way to do this is, as you go through life, try not to have specific goal weights in mind because they will always be moving targets and your body will naturally fluctuate as you grow and age, so what was considered a healthy goal at 14 while your hormones are still adjusting will not be the same goal when you pass 18 and develop into a woman. Instead, try to focus on maintaining your recovery related goals such as eating intuitively, spending less time checking your body in the mirror, and reducing your anxiety around certain foods.

Wearing what you feel comfortable in is more important than ever and it is recommended by many anorexia support workers that you get rid of all of your "sick clothes;" why not donate them to charity? This will help you to remove any nostalgia around your eating disorder and move forward with a more healthy idea of how your current body looks. Some people will take pride in their weight gain, seeing it as a sign of achievement, and celebrate by wearing figure hugging clothes, whereas others will prefer to continue wearing loose fitting clothing so that they don't feel the tight fabric on their skin. Whatever you decide to do from here on, make sure you feel okay in your body and mind; that's all that matters.

You may also need to come to terms with the fact that some of your friends may no longer be around or beneficial for your life, and that's fine. Growing apart from each other suggests that they are on different paths and it doesn't necessarily mean that they are bad people. Just be open to creating new healthy connections instead. As for the friends who have stuck by you throughout your treatment and recovery and continue to value you in the way you deserve, they will be over the moon! They will have got their friend back and will be looking forward to eventually doing all the things they'd done with you before again. They, with the support of your school, could also help you with any part of education you may have missed so that you are prepared for independent and working life.

My life after anorexia is much more relaxed. I enjoy wearing clothes that compliment my new shape and I no longer worry about what others think about it. I also have the confidence to eat foods that make me feel happy and fulfilled, without feeling sad or guilty afterwards–I just try to make sure that I don't get overly full. For example, I'd probably still order a chicken salad from McCalister's because it is light, but now I'd be comfortable enough to add a sugar cookie. That way, I nourish my body healthily with the vegetables and protein while feeding my not-so-secret sugar addiction with dessert! I'm also happier to go out for meals in the company of others and try new cuisines like Japanese fried rice and shrimp. I now pay more attention to how food makes me feel and the positive associations attached to it as well as its value to me in the long-term to help me decide whether I eat it or not. So I'd say that I have a much healthier relationship with food than I ever have done.

A HEALTHY RELATIONSHIP WITH FOOD

Registered dietitian, nutritionist, and founder of Eat with Knowledge, Jennifer McGurk, says that having a positive relationship with food is the best way to keep eating disorders at bay. She suggests that the more you respect food and value all the good it can do for your body, the less likely it will be that you will struggle to consume it. It has nothing to do with the quality of your diet, but rather understanding and monitoring how and why you choose the foods you eat, which is essential for limiting stress and maintaining your recovery. McGurk also notes that if you have a varied diet, you will tend to be healthier and brave enough to try new food as you get older too. By experimenting with meals in this way, you will develop distress tolerance and realize that you are strong enough to ignore or push through any feelings of disgust or fear when it comes to food. So this is your cue to be more open to trying new dishes and flavors; from spicy Indian food to indulgent ice creams, the array of flavors and textures that await is immense. You could start by challenging yourself to eat one new dish per month to discover what works and feels good for you.

Food is not an enemy, but something that should be enjoyed and appreciated. It is the source of life that enables us to not only function well, but also brings happiness, energy, and success. Unlike animals that eat purely for survival, humans also eat food as a celebration of culture or tradition, a source of joy or pleasure, and it often acts as a tool for bringing people together, which are all beautiful aspects of a fulfilling life. You are not defined by what you eat, so you should be able to honestly and confidently give yourself unconditional permission to enjoy food and feel satisfied at the end of a meal. Eating what you enjoy shouldn't make you feel guilty as the occasional treat won't do you any harm and there is no such thing as good or bad food; it's simply about moderation. For example, some may say that candy is 'bad,' but eating a packet of candy once a week won't make you an unhealthy person. Eating a packet of candy every day, however, will be detrimental to your physical and mental health, so just being aware of what and how much you are eating is key. Furthermore, it's important to pay attention to the language you use surrounding food, so even words like 'clean,' 'junk,' 'forbidden,' or 'superfoods' should be avoided because they can subconsciously influence how you respond and treat these items and make you restrict your diet again.

Flexibility around what you will and won't eat will also be beneficial when trying to start a new life post-anorexia. You are no longer constrained by food or living rules, so keeping your mind open will give you a better eating experience. For example, if you go out for a meal and the restaurant no longer serves your favorite fruit salad on the dessert menu, try to be open to ordering the chocolate fudge cake instead; it could be just as nice if not better! Thinking positively when your food plans don't go as you'd hoped will reduce the stress associated around meal times significantly and make you less likely to fall into obsessive habits again.

Making your own dishes from scratch can also be a great way to improve your relationship with food going forward. It can be a time during which you connect with your parents and siblings to encourage healthy attitudes towards food for the whole family and by engaging all of your senses when handling, cutting, mashing, and preparing food, you will start to learn about the raw ingredients. You can also control your portion size and you'll be more aware of hygiene and food safety if this is something you'd been anxious about when in the throes of anorexia.

This new attitude towards food won't develop overnight, and it may come and go, so it's something that you will probably have to keep working at for the rest of your life. But now is the time to start facing previous fears head on and use all that you've learned so far to help you keep winning the ongoing battles.

YOUR BRILLIANT BODY

Although it may not seem like it to you, your body has done and will continue to do so much good for you. Anorexia may have hurt some parts or made you feel like you've been let down by your mind, but the fact that you are still standing is a testament to you and your body's hard work and ability to heal. The human body is brilliant and resilient, so now you should appreciate it and look after it in the best way you can.

Body scans are one way Mindful magazine recommends people could come to love and understand their bodies better (Smookler, 2019). This has nothing to do with machines or hospitals but rather the mind in which the person quiets any anxious or negative thoughts and tunes into any aches, pains, or tensions as they 'scan' around the body. They then inhale and exhale deeply to release any areas of discomfort and slowly retune their body in a more comfortable way. It is a form of meditation that can take just 30 minutes to complete and will leave you feeling positive and in control.

Keeping active is another way to recognize and celebrate your brilliant body. If you enjoyed going to the gym and being active before your recovery, don't be afraid to return to this pastime, but this time, do it because you love your body rather than because you hate or want to change it. Build muscle so that you can easily carry your book and shopping bags after a day out with your friends. Improve your stamina by going for walks and runs so that you can rejoin your local volleyball team and play with your younger siblings. With the right state of mind, restarting your activities can feel liberating and exciting.

Your eating disorder voice may not have completely disappeared but the more you appreciate what your body does and do things that it likes, the quieter your dysmorphia will be and the louder your body's confident voice will be, because ultimately it's about how you feel, not how you look.

Your body is an instrument not an ornament. –Jennifer McGurk

AFTERWORD

Going through anorexia nervosa is not an easy ride and it has probably led you to do, say, and think things that you would have never imagined before. You've been overwhelmed and triggered by things you thought were within your comfort zone, been upset by situations that barely affect your peers, and have changed your behavior in ways that have potentially severely hurt and altered your body. All of this is a lot to handle as a teenager and unfortunately shows that our minds are capable of convincing us that unhealthy behavior is positive. But by using the insights and tips in this book, you will be able to override these thoughts and urges, heal, and become a happier and more self-assured person. Every girl's body and mind deserves to be healthy and looked after with the utmost care because you only get one of each and they are truly precious. Also remember that suffering from anorexia is nobody's fault and there is nothing that you could have done to deserve it as a punishment. It's just one of those phenomena that some people are unfortunate enough to experience.

AFTERWORD

Now that you've acknowledged that you have anorexia, be proud of yourself for taking that step and try to look forward to a time where you can say that you *had* an eating disorder but are now thriving. Focus on being able to say goodbye to the old version of yourself and welcome a life that no longer revolves around food, weight, looks, control, and meticulous meal planning. Recover at your own pace and remember that your family, friends, partner, school, and treatment team (if you already have one) all want you to do well too.

There are, of course, some devastating anorexia journeys that don't have happy endings, so it is a condition that needs to be taken seriously. But, there are thousands of other stories like mine that do end in recovery, so continue to seek these out for inspiration and motivation if you ever feel overwhelmed. If I can get through it, there's no reason why you can't too.

BIBLIOGRAPHY

Anorexia Nervosa. (n.d.). Cleveland Clinic. https://my.clevelandclinic.org/health/diseases/9794-anorexia-nervosa

Bullying and eating disorders. (n.d.). National Eating Disorders Association. https://www.nationaleatingdisorders.org/bullying

Campbell, L. (2019, September 14). *Why men avoid going to the doctor.* Healthline. https://www.healthline.com/health-news/why-so-many-men-avoid-doctors

Clifton, T. (2022, April 13). *Exercise for teenagers: How much they need, and how to fit it in.* Healthline. https://www.healthline.com/health/fitness/exercise-for-teenagers

Cyberbullying: twenty crucial statistics for 2020. (2022, March 29). Security.org. https://www.security.org/resources/cyberbullying-facts-statistics/

Davenport, N. (n.d.). *10 ways to cope with a relapse in eating disorder recovery.* National Eating Disorders Association. https://www.nationaleatingdisorders.org/blog/10-ways-cope-with-relapse-eating-disorder-recovery

Eating disorders soared in lockdown, experts warn. (2021, June 16). BBC News. https://www.bbc.co.uk/news/uk-scotland-57488220

Eating disorders: what is the prognosis? (2019). National Institute for Health and Care Excellence. https://cks.nice.org.uk/topics/eating-disorders/background-information/prognosis/

Eating disorders (young people) - school & studying. (2018, October). Healthtalk.org. https://healthtalk.org/eating-disorders/school-studying

FEAST: Support and resources for families affected by eating disorders. (n.d.). FEAST. https://www.feast-ed.org

5 big benefits of creative expression. (2019, May 15). Brightwater Group. https://brightwatergroup.com/news-articles/5-big-benefits-of-creative-expression/

Floyd, K. (n.d.). *Do I need inpatient eating disorder treatment?* Walden Behavioral Care. https://www.waldeneatingdisorders.com/blog/do-you-need-inpatient-eating-disorder-treatment/

Grubiak, K. (2022, January 27). *Restoring nutritional health in anorexia nervosa.* Verywell Mind. https://www.verywellmind.com/restoring-nutritional-health-in-anorexia-nervosa-recovery-4115081

Haines, A. (2021, April 27). *From "Instagram face" to "Snapchat dysmorphia": how beauty filters are changing the way we see ourselves.* Forbes. https://www.-

forbes.com/sites/annahaines/2021/04/27/from-instagram-face-to-snapchat-dysmorphia-how-beauty-filters-are-changing-the-way-we-see-ourselves/?sh=54bab6114eff

The importance of family support while working toward eating disorder recovery. (n.d.). Oliver-Pyatt Centers. https://www.oliverpyattcenters.com/importance-of-family-support/

Is there a link between social media and eating disorders? (2019, May 23). Magnolia Creek Center. https://www.magnoliacreek.com/resources/blog/social-media-and-eating-disorders/

Jarman, H. K., Treneman-Evans, G., & Halliwell, E. (2021). "I didn't want to say something and them to go outside and tell everyone": The acceptability of a dissonance-based body image intervention among adolescent girls in the UK. *Body Image,* (38), 80–84. https://doi.org/10.1016/j.bodyim.2021.03.011

Jones, G. (2021, June 29). *Help your teen with an eating disorder get enough sleep.* More Love. https://more-love.org/2021/06/29/teen-eating-disorder-sleep/

Justice, J., & Karpen, E. (2021, February 10). *In a "lighter equals faster" culture, runners must combat a culture of disordered eating.* Columbia Daily Spectator. https://www.columbiaspectator.com/the-eye/2021/02/10/in-a-lighter-equals-faster-culture-runners-must-combat-a-culture-of-disordered-eating/

Kaufman, S. B. (2019, December 12). *Taking sex differences in personality seriously.* Scientific American. https://blogs.scientificamerican.com/beautiful-minds/taking-sex-differences-in-personality-seriously/

Leigh, S. (2019, November 19). *Many patients with anorexia nervosa get better, but complete recovery elusive to most.* UCSF. https://www.ucsf.edu/news/2019/11/416006/many-patients-anorexia-nervosa-get-better-complete-recovery-elusive-most

Loneliness and eating disorders. (2019, July 26). Center for Discovery. https://centerfordiscovery.com/blog/loneliness-eating-disorders/

McGurk, J. (2020, January 16). *20 tips for intuitive eating and eating disorder recovery in 2020.* Eat with Knowledge. https://eatwithknowledge.com/20-tips-intuitive-eating-eating-disorder-recovery/

Mensi, M. M., Balottin, L., Rogantini, C., Orlandi, M., Galvani, M., Figini, S., Chiappedi, M., & Balottin, U. (2020). Focus on family functioning in anorexia nervosa: New perspectives using the lausanne trilogue play. *Psychiatry Research,* (288), 112968. https://doi.org/10.1016/j.psychres.2020.112968

Misluk, E. (n.d.). *The benefits of art therapy in eating disorder treatment.* Eating Disorders Review. https://eatingdisordersreview.com/the-benefits-of-art-therapy-in-eating-disorder-treatment/

Muhlheim, L. (2020, October 10). *How we set recovery weights.* Eating Disorder Therapy LA. https://www.eatingdisordertherapyla.com/how-we-set-recovery-weights/

Muhlheim, L. (2020, May 22). *Why full anorexia recovery is crucial for brain health.* Verywell Mind. https://www.verywellmind.com/brain-starvation-and-recovery-in-anorexia-nervosa-1138303

My child has an eating disorder - is it my fault? (2020, September 11). Eating Recovery Center. https://www.eatingrecoverycenter.com/resources/child-has-eating-disorder-my-fault

Parker, L. L., & Harriger, J. A. (2020). Eating disorders and disordered eating behaviors in the LGBT population: a review of the literature. *Journal of Eating Disorders*, (8), 51. https://doi.org/10.1186/s40337-020-00327-y

Pegg Frates, E. (2021, October 5). *Did we really gain weight during the pandemic?* Harvard Health Publishing. https://www.health.harvard.edu/blog/did-we-really-gain-weight-during-the-pandemic-202110052606

Pipitone, N. (n.d.). *Can bullying lead to an eating disorder?* Walden Behavioral Care. https://www.waldeneatingdisorders.com/blog/can-bullying-lead-to-an-eating-disorder/

Priya, A., Applewhite, B., Au, K., & Oyeleye, O., Walton, E., Norton, C., Patsalos, O., Cardi, V., & Himmerich H (2021, June 2). Attitudes surrounding music of patients with anorexia nervosa: a survey-based mixed-methods analysis. *Frontiers in Psychiatry*, (12), 639202 https://www.frontiersin.org/articles/10.3389/fpsyt.2021.639202/full

The pros and cons of friendships in eating disorder treatment. (n.d.). Walden Behavioral Care. https://www.waldeneatingdisorders.com/blog/the-pros-and-cons-of-friendships-in-eating-disorder-treatment/

Rehman, A. (2022, February 15). *Eating disorder statistics 2022.* Singlecare. https://www.singlecare.com/blog/news/eating-disorder-statistics/

Rittenhouse, M. (2021, August 17). *Eating disorders and anxiety.* Eating Disorder Hope. https://www.eatingdisorderhope.com/treatment-for-eating-disorders/co-occurring-dual-diagnosis/anxiety

Schurrer, M.-E. (2020, January 23). *Dark side of body image in competitive sports.* HealthyPlace. https://www.healthyplace.com/blogs/survivinged/2020/1/dark-side-of-body-image-in-competitive-sports

Smith, M., Robinson, L., & Segal, J. (2020, September). *Eating disorder treatment and recovery.* HelpGuide.org. https://www.helpguide.org/articles/eating-disorders/eating-disorder-treatment-and-recovery.htm

Smookler, E. (2019, April 11). *Beginner's body scan meditation.* Mindful. https://www.mindful.org/beginners-body-scan-meditation/

Suni, E. (2022, June 10). *Eating disorders and sleep.* Sleep Foundation. https://www.sleepfoundation.org/mental-health/eating-disorders-and-sleep

TEDx Talks. (2017, October 17). *Nostalgia | Lene Marie Fossen & Morten Krogvold | TEDxArendal* [Video]. YouTube. https://www.youtube.com/watch?v=bOkSQJQIRV0

Teens and social media use: what's the impact? (2022, February 26). Mayo Clinic. https://www.mayoclinic.org/healthy-lifestyle/tween-and-teen-health/in-depth/teens-and-social-media-use/art-20474437

Printed in Great Britain
by Amazon